Kathy Acker's previous publications include *Blood and Guts in High School*, *Great Expectation* and *My Mother: Demonology*. Novelist, essayist and critic, her work has been received with wide acclaim in the United States, Britain and Europe. *Kirkus Reviews* writes, 'There's a haunting method to Acker's "madness": a rough, raw, erudite wail against the postmodern loss of meaning and emotion.'

Bodies

of Work

essays by

Kathy Acker

The author gratefully acknowledges the original publishers of these essays.

Library of Congress Catalog Card Number: LC 95-72974

A catalogue record for this book is available from the British Library on request

First published in 1997 by
Serpent's Tail, 4 Blackstock Mews, London N4
and 180 Varick Street, 10th floor, New York, NY 10014

Set in Sabon by Avon Dataset, Bidford-on-Avon
Printed in Great Britain by Mackays of Chatham

Contents

Preface

I am introducing these essays by announcing that what I have to say about them is strange.

When the publishers of this book asked me to write a preface, I replied, "I'm not sure I like my essays."

Questioning this immediate emotional response, I arrived at a query that was more interesting to me than one about the value of my journalistic and theoretical work. Why bother to write at all?

I am sitting on a narrow bed in a very brown hotel room somewhere at the edge of Russia. Yeltsin is ill. Beyond translucent window curtains, the sky looks dark even though it is afternoon. There is not a hint of rain. Winter has begun its reign.

Over lunch this afternoon, one of my foreign publishers told me that the apocalypse is approaching. Men are becoming less humane, more openly and guiltlessly violent. There is a new group of predators in the world; look, what is now happening in Belgium. Soon society will be divided into predators and victims. As for women, they can harm their own children which, in the past, they were unable to do due to some genetic structuring. Both sexes are showing less and less desire to procreate, even to have sex.

These dissolvings, which are happening now, will be interrupted by an unexpected catastrophe. Something will take place in the electro-magnetic fields: all electricity will cease. Only the top members of organizations such as the army, which army or armies wasn't mentioned, will survive, for they have contingency plans that anticipate such events.

Was it a Gnostic view that every level of reality reflects every other, that each world and each mind mirror each other?

I replied that whatever the scenario or scenarios, we certainly are living in a time, and geography, dominated by radical change. So radical that the pace of time is increasing to such a degree that time seems to be threatening to disappear.

All of us are faced, as perhaps we never before have been, by death.

Why write in such a time as this? I am writing down this question.

My first question, about the value, literary and otherwise, of the essays you're about to read, is relatively easy to approach. For me writing is freedom. Therein lies (my) identity. I prefer writing fiction to essays because there is more freedom in fiction and so, I question my essays. To be precise, essay-writing seems, at least at first glance, tied to expression. The problem with expression is that it is too narrow a basis for writing, for it is pinned to knowledge, knowledge which is mainly rational. I trust neither my ability to know nor what I think I know. Moreover, the excitement of writing, for me, is that of a journey into strangeness: to write down what one thinks one knows is to destroy possibilities for joy.

I'm not arguing that writing is wedded to nonsense and not to communication; obviously to use language is to enter the world; rather I am hoping that communication need not be reduced to expression.

What else can communication be? All of me screams out: vision.

My unease with the essay form has led me to try to play, even to destroy, the form. When writing essays I have used chance structurally: by viewing subjects through the lens of supposedly unrelated subjects; by reading a text's content only through its structure; by reading a non-literary text, say a painting, by trying to imitate it literally, in words.

Common literary techniques. I am not satisfied. I come to my second question: why bother to write in times such as these?

Do I write to express what is made or to make? I seem to have chosen the latter, the modernist way.

But it is not so simple. To oppose expression and a Joycean making is to situate oneself in dualism and so to remain bereft of all that is visionary.

I have written down some of what I think I know: again, I'm not satisfied.

I'm sitting on this bed, between writing spurts, idly beginning to read a novel by Maurice Blanchot entitled (in English) *The Most High*. In his introduction to this book, Allan Stoekl quotes a letter from Georges Bataille to Alexandre Kojeve, December 1937. "I grant (as a likely supposition)," muses Bataille, "that from now on history is ended (except for the denouement). However, I picture things differently (. . . it certainly doesn't seem impossible that, in some very distant time, everything will begin again.)"

The problem, it suddenly comes to me, with this end of the world, with the apocalypse is that the mind is so powerful that what is thought comes to pass.

Stoekl is continuing to explain Kojeve, Kojeve's influence on French intellectuals such as Bataille. That Kojeve's explication of Hegel's *Phenomenology* turned philosophers and writers such as Sartre, Merleau-Ponty, Lacan, Bataille and Queneau into Hegelians. As did Hegel, they assumed that human history is going somewhere, that it has an endpoint, a goal.

I am thinking that the more I write, the more convinced I am that writing, be it about time, is time. Is change, rhythm. Those movements of time. Need writing be only one kind of time, linear time, that form called history? Need writing end? If history, that kind of time, does end, what kind or kinds of time will there be? Since such time wouldn't be linear, it might be happening now. If writing is time, as I suspect, what would writing look like outisde of linear narrative or time? What does this writing look like outside of linear narrative or time?

I am thinking about the difference between history and myth.

Or between expression and vision. The need for narrative and the simultaneous need to escape the prison-house of the story—to misquote. What is the essay in this situation?

I question the works you're about to read.

1997

1.

On Art and Artists

William Burroughs's Realism

From the time of my high school days, I have known, in the way that one knows the streets of one's city and the laws of one's culture, the names of those in the pantheon of great living American writers. The big men. Norman Mailer, macho of machos; Philip Roth; John Cheever; etc. Perhaps at the head of the class, Saul Bellow. There weren't many, any, women. These heroes criticized United States society as it needed to be criticized in cultured tones.

The problem with both their criticism and their manner of criticism is that neither American society nor American culture is cultured. To analyze and sound the faults of the American way of life in educated bourgeois terms and modes is a spurious exercise. For in its cultural, social, and political behavior, the United States resembles a giant baby, perhaps mongoloid, almost uneducated and increasingly uninterested in questioning and education, who not maliciously but unknowingly breaks everything it meets as it crawls around in chaotic paths. According to Piaget, a baby regards the world as an extension of his or her own identity; for a baby, there is no other.

Pretend that there is a distinct entity named *self* and a different entity named *other* or *world*. Define *insanity* as the situation when there occurs a nonnegotiable disparity between the self's version of the world and the world. According to this definition, American culture now is insane. Well-measured language, novels which structurally depend on the Aristotelian continuities, on any formal continuities, cannot describe, much less criticize, such culture.

In terms of content and formally, William Burroughs's writings are those of discontinuity and dissolution. Both represented time and the books' temporal structures are fractured; time juts into and becomes space; humans melt into cartoonlike characteristics and parts of bodies gone haywire; the quality of humanity seems to be green mush or resolves into unheard-of mutations. Due to these psychotic realities, Burroughs, in his writing, was able to portray futures which are now our present.

Regarding the natures of truth and reality in nonbourgeois fiction, in Burroughs's fiction:

The following section from *The Soft Machine* by William Burroughs, published first in 1961, is fiction:

> *Carl walked through a carnival city along canals where giant pink salamanders and goldfish stirred slowly; penny arcades, tattoo booths, massage parlors, sideshows, blue movies, processions, floats, performers, pitchmen to the sky.*

The following is a true story: While I was sitting with several friends in a bar, one of them said that his girlfriend had recently left him. "Coney Island in the dead season. A cumulation of buildings aged by time and neglect into some substance the color of dog-shit. Here live old people on welfare. And empty machines: roller-coasters, Ferris wheels whose cars spin opposite to the wheel's turn. Guaranteed to create nausea just as artists create . . . art.

"During the winter, the season of the dead, some of the geeks who worked the machines and fun-houses remain living in their holes, next to tarred and salty sands.

"Just after my girlfriend left me, I came here. It was drizzling, as it always does in the heart. Boarded-up windows, old men sitting behind them, waiting for nothing. A dead sea.

"As I walked past some brown building, a hunchback beckoned to me. Called me by name.

"'I have something for you.'

"I followed the old man into an apartment that was almost a shack. Down a set of narrow wood stairs. It was so dark, I was scared of falling. So at first, I couldn't hear the creep's mumbles.

"'Can't keep it anymore . . . my prize possession. Illegal. Might as well declare all of us . . . no use . . .'

"I clearly heard him tell me that he would sell it to me for five hundred dollars.

"Now I was in his room. Filled with all sorts of junk: upside-down chairs, stripper outfits, wigs, cracked mirrors, dead cigarettes. Scattered. A large glass jar stood on a table in the back of the room.

"Inside the jar, in liquid, tiny fingers splayed, some of them pointing to me. Its . . . his . . . her . . . mouth was open like a fish.

"I gave him five hundred bucks.

"As I walked with that jar under my arm, I knew that my girlfriend had given me a baby."

What is fiction is that which will become actual. In his novels, Burroughs saw the society around him so clearly, he announced the future. Writing that seemed radical when it appeared today looks like journalism. In other words: today in the United States, we are living in the worlds of Burroughs's novels. Pray that the wild boys will help us escape.

The language of our media who dictate our political and social actualities is that of (false) continuity and (always partially false) fact: simple declarative sentences, as little use of ambiguity as possible, no dwelling within verbal sensuousness. Burroughs fights this post-bourgeois language with poetry: images, dangling clauses, all that lingers at the edges of the unsaid, that leads to and through dreams.

As Burroughs has said: without dreams, our desires, especially sexual desires, we will die.

1990

Postmodernism

I'm unaccustomed, and reluctant, to write about why I write the ways I do, but a few paragraphs by Bill Berkson on "postmodernism" which Lyn Hejinian and Barrett Watten just sent me have so enraged me that I am trying to write something. I will be too simple, trying to figure out the un-figurable. This is why language is always fiction and true.

"Culture doesn't account for actual practice"—Bill Berkson. I write with words which are given me. If it wasn't for certain community consensus as to the meanings and usages of words, words would be nonsense. Language, then, deeply is discourse: when I use language, I am given meaning and I give meaning back to the community. "Culture" is one way by which a community attempts to bring its past up out of senselessness and to find in dream and imagination possibilities for action. When culture isn't this, there's something wrong in the community, the society.

Political, economic and moral forces are major determiners of meanings and values in a society. Thus, when I use words, any words, I am always taking part in the constructing of the political, economic, and moral community in which my discourse is taking place. All aspects of language—denotation, sound, style, syntax, grammar, etc.—are politically, economically and morally coded. In this sense, there's no escaping content. Whenever someone, the literati, the professors, declares that there is such a thing as "total ornament," that "art is pure," what they are saying is that the rich own culture, discourse, and probably the world. If this seems like a non sequitur, you figure it out.

Whenever I engage in discourse, I am using given meanings and values, changing them and giving them back. A community, a society is always being constructed in discourse if and when discourse—including art—is allowed. Societies whose economies are set, fascist ones for instance, place little or no emphasis on free discourse, on art. Of course art, then, is trivial. The rich want to stay rich.

Language always occurs in the present because it makes the present, because it's active.

We are now, in the United States and in England, living in a world in which ownership is becoming more and more set: The rich stay rich; the poor stay dead. Death-in-life. The only social mobility left occurs in terms of appearance: things no longer change hands. But fashion is not purely ornamental: it is political. All signs nowadays point either to the world of the "haves" or to the homeless Chicanos on the L.A. downtown streets. There is no more right-wing versus working class: there is only appearance and disappearance, those people who appear in the media and those people who have disappeared from the possibility of any sort of home. In such a society as ours the only possible chance for change, for mobility, for political, economic, and moral flow lies in the tactics of guerrilla warfare, in the use of fictions, of language.

Postmodernism, then, for the moment, is a useful perspective and tactic. If we don't live for and in the, this, moment, we do not live.

2. A Few Notes on Two of My Books

For weeks, months, now, I've been avoiding writing this: I have an almost uncontrollable desire not to talk about my writing. Why? If I had something to say about my writing outside my writing, something written which occurred outside my writing, my writing wouldn't be sufficient or adequate.

Everything is thrown into my writing.

I'll begin talking about someone else's writing. Living in England, I keep returning to American literature. That tradition. At this moment, to the books of William Burroughs. Unlike most of the writing in the contemporary novels of this country, Burroughs's writing is "immediate." "Immediate" has something to do with the sentence "I want to read something that means something to me." Most English contemporary novels, forgetting those of Ballard, bore me. At best, they entertain. But they don't talk to me. Burroughs never bores, for he and the other writers I think of as in "that tradition," "the other tradition," "the non-acceptable literary tradition," "the tradition of those books which were hated when they were written and subsequently became literary history," "the black tradition," "the tradition of political writing as opposed to propaganda" (de Sade would head this list) (here I am not talking about American literary tradition), do what Poe said a writer should do. They present the human heart naked so that our world, for a second, explodes into flames. This human heart is not only the individual heart: the American literary tradition of Thoreau, Emerson, even Miller, presents the individual and communal heart as a unity. Any appearance of the individual heart is a political occurrence.

Writers such as Burroughs, Selby, etc., have always been attacked on personal rather than on literary grounds.

"Marginal," "experimental," and "avant-garde" are often words used to describe texts in this other tradition. Not because writing such as Burroughs's or Genet's is marginal, but because our society, through the voice of its literary society, cannot bear immediacy, the truth, especially the political truth.

I've never been sure about the need for literary criticism. If a work is immediate enough, alive enough, the proper response isn't to be academic, to write about it, but to use it, to go on. By using each other, each other's texts, we keep on living, imagining, making, fucking, and we fight this society to death.

But I'm a good girl: I was told to write about my own texts so I shall do so.

In 1979 I wrote "New York City in 1979," published by Anne Turyn in her series named "Top Stories." In this short story I did two things. First, I took my present environment, the Lower East Side in New York City, and described it, its society. I hated the life which I was living at that time; I hated the society; I didn't differentiate between the two. I thought that if my friends and our society didn't find a way for adequate change, we would die and quickly. Some of us did die. I wanted radical change, however it had to come. At the same time I was aware that writing changes nothing on the larger political scale. One reason for this, of course, is that those who are most oppressed are often either illiterate or rarely read. Literature, especially novels, is written by and for the owning or the educated populace. Here is one reason why the novel is one of the most conservative art forms in our century. I wanted change, but I had no adequate tools or weapons, I was, at best, a writer.

If writing cannot and writing must change things, I thought to myself, logically of course, writing *will* change things magically. Magic operates metaphorically. So: I will take one text, New York City, the life of my friends, and change this text by placing another text on top of it.

I do know that writing or making is magic. I'm not referring to "magic realism."

As my second text, I took a story about Charles Baudelaire and Jeanne Duval. I believe, a true story. Jeanne Duval had been an incredibly beautiful black woman. Baudelaire gave her syphilis and then fell in love with her. Baudelaire said in his notebook in 1846:

Her beauty has vanished under the dreadful crust of smallpox, like foliage under the ice of winter. Still moved by her long sufferings and the fits of the disease, you gaze sadly at the ineffaceable stigmata on the beloved convalescent's body; suddenly you hear echoing in your eyes a dying tune executed by the raving bow of Paganini, and this sympathetic tune speaks to you of yourself, seems to describe your whole inner poem of lost hopes. Thenceforth the traces of smallpox will be part of your happiness.

Here was a model of change: ugliness changed through worse ugliness, even destruction, into love.

I placed the second text on top of the first text, crudely. You do what you have to do however you have to do it.

For me, the myth of Daedalus defines fiction, literature. According to Robert Graves, Daedalus was a highly skilled craftsman. His king, Minos of Cretan Cnossus, honored him until he learned that Daedalus had helped his (Minos's) wife fuck a white bull. Then Minos made Crete Daedalus's prison.

Daedalus escaped prison by his art. He made wings for himself and his son. His son got too high, flew too high, soared into the sun, and drowned.

Art is this certain kind of making. A writer makes reality, a writer is a kind of journalist, a magic one.

Does "make" mean "create"?

When I was about fifteen and living in New York City, I had a boyfriend, P. Adams Sitney, who was making films, working at the Mekas's Film Co-Op, and editing his own film magazine. He introduced me to Jackson MacLow, Robert Kelly, and to the work of Charles Olson. At the time I felt confused, that I was understanding nothing, but something must have filtered in. Robert Kelly and his first wife, Joby, were painting Pound's dictum "MAKE IT NEW" on stones, poundstones. I'm not sure if my memories are historically valid; I never am. I remember that Robert Creeley taught that a writer, a poet, is a real writer when he (or she) finds his own voice. (Back then, "he" was important enough to include "she.")

When I was either twenty or twenty-one, I again moved away from New York City, back to San Diego where I had done my last two years of college and first two years of graduate school. I apprenticed myself to David Antin. That is, I sat on his doorstep and babysat for his kid. Blaise, the kid, and I got along great. Our favorite game was "Criminals"; a sample question: "Would you rather hold up a small bank in Kentucky or poison a rich creep who's already dying?" "MAKE IT NEW." I wanted to be a writer; I didn't want to do anything else; but I couldn't find my own voice. The act of writing for me was the most pleasurable thing in the world. Just writing. Why did I have to find my own voice and where was it? I hated my fathers.

These old feelings, questionings, and intuitions in me have done nothing but grow. I now wonder where the idea or the ideology of creativity started. Shakespeare and company certainly stole from, copied each other's writings. Before them, the Greeks didn't bother making up any new stories. I suspect that the ideology of creativity started when the bourgeoisie—when they rose up in all their splendor, as the history books put it—made a capitalistic market-place for books. Today a writer earns money or a living by selling copyright, ownership to words. We all do it, we writers, this scam, because we need to earn money, only most don't admit it's a scam. Nobody *really* owns nothing. Dead men don't fuck.

There's another part to this argument. For a while, back in my early days of writing, I looked for a voice, a self. I placed "true" autobiography next to "false" autobiography. I learned two things. First, in fiction, there is no "true" or "false" in social-realist terms. Fiction is "true" or real when it makes. Second, if there is a self, it isn't Hegel's subject or the centralized phallic I/eye. If there is a self, it's probably the world. All is real. When I placed "true" autobiography next to "false" autobiography, everything was real. Phallic identity's another scam that probably had to do with capitalistic ownership.

Fiction is magic because everything is magic: the world is always making itself. When you make fiction, you dip into this process. But no one, writer or politician, is more powerful than the world: you can make, but you don't create. Only the incredible egotism that resulted from a belief in phallic centricism could have come up with the notion of creativity.

Of course, a woman is the muse. If she were the maker instead of the muse and opened her mouth, she would blast the notion of poetic creativity apart.

When I copy, I don't "appropriate." I just do what gives me most pleasure: write. As the Gnostics put it, when two people fuck, the whole world fucks.

In his introduction to *Imaginary Magnitude*, Stanislaw Lem talks about this "cult of the new," about modernism. We were promised, he says, that by following out the new, we could, traversing carrying geographies, arrive at landscapes never before seen. We could learn what wasn't before known and, perhaps, the unknowable. In actuality, by following the "cult of the new," we have exchanged "one old, spontaneous, and therefore unconscious bondage for a new one"; we have not "cut the fetters," but have made freedom into a law.

"I myself," Lem continues, "crave a different basis for heresy and rebellion."

What basis? Right now, Lem argues, art is on the point of being totally useless, of not being, for we are living in a society that marginalizes, distrusts both art and its artists. We are also living in a society that seems bent on its own self-destruction. Though Lem is speaking about the other side of what used to be the "Iron Curtain," he could well be speaking about our world.

Unfortunately, our society's self-destruction would involve us. So the artist finds himself or herself in a peculiar position. The artist doesn't need to find out the limits of his or her medium, to "make it new"; the artist, though politically and socially powerless, marginalized, must find the ways for all of our survival.

Method has become supremely, politically important. For example, the novelist who writes about the poor Cambridge vicar who can't deal with his homosexuality is giving us no tools for survival. Whereas William Burroughs's writing methods, his uses of psychic research, are weapons in the fight for our own happiness.

When I began writing my most recently published novel, *Empire of the Senseless*, I heard myself saying to myself, repeatedly: "You can't change this society. You know this. The fucking hippies didn't change anything; maybe it's worse now even than in the McCarthy days. But despair stinks. Living every day by wanting to die. How can happiness be possible in this society?"

When I wrote my first book, *Politics*, I was living in a society that was politically and socially hypocritical. According to the media back then, politicians were men who said sweet things to babies and neither adultery nor drug abuse ever came near a middle-class white American home.

Perhaps our society is now in a "post-cynical" phase. Certainly, I thought as I started *Empire*, there's no more need to deconstruct, to take apart perceptual habits, to reveal the frauds on which our society's living. We now have to find somewhere to go, a belief, a myth. Somewhere real. In *Rebel Without a Cause* the kids are desperately looking for a place so they can live.

Empire of the Senseless is my first attempt to find a myth, a place, not the myth, the place.

As it was being written this book divided itself into three sections. The first part, "Elegy for the World of the Fathers," is a description of the society which is defined by the oedipal taboo. The oedipal myth, after all, is not only one story out of many, but also just part of one myth, the Theban cycle.

To learn how the oedipal society looks, I turned to several texts, mainly to those by the Marquis de Sade and by Freud. Freud, for obvious reasons. At one point I was going to give all my characters the names of Freud's patients. (Only Dr. Shreber survived.) Anything for a bad joke. To the Marquis de Sade because he shed so much light on our Western sexual politics that his name is still synonymous with an activity more appropriately named "Reaganism." Something of that sort. As I've said, I never write anything new.

In "Alone," the second part of *Empire*, I tried to describe a society not defined by the oedipal taboo. That is, by phallic centricity and total domination on the political, economic, social, and personal levels. Some of my texts for this section were ones by Jean Genet and Pierre Guyotat, for both these writers, perhaps partly because of their sexualities, have described other than oedipal relationships. Have described different nexes between power, sexuality, and politics. Guyotat's writing was influenced by his experiences in the Algerian war. I thought, as I wrote this section, that today, as the "Great Powers," as they were formerly known, meet and meld economically, then culturally, as more and more of the known world goes Coca-Cola and McDonalds, only the Muslim world resists. A French friend of mind who frequently travels to South Africa just told me that one town which he often visits ten years ago had twenty churches and one mosque. Today, the opposite is true. I thought, for Westerners today, for us, the other is now Muslim. In my book, when the Algerians take over Paris, I have a society not defined by the oedipal taboo.

As I wrote this second part, I learned that it is impossible to have, to live in a hypothetical, not utopian but perhaps freer, society if one does not actually inhabit such a world. One must be where one is. The body does not lie. Language, if it is not propaganda or media blab, is the body; with such language lies are not possible. If lies were possible, there would be no reason to write fiction.

Specifically, I live in a world which is at least partly defined by the multinationals, the CIA, etc. Nowhere else. So the CIA kept invading the Paris in *Empire*; for this section I used various journalistic texts. As I put these texts together, I realized, as I did years ago, that the hippies had been mistaken: they had thought that they could successfully oppose American postcapitalism by a lie, by creating a utopian society. But the body is real: if one, anyone, lives in hell, one is hell. Dualisms such as good/evil are not real and only reality works.

By the end of "Alone" I found myself at the end of the second part of a dialectical argument. I was back to my original question: In a society defined by phallic centricism or by prison, how is it possible to be happy?

The last section of *Empire* begins with the text of *Huckleberry Finn*, one of the main texts about freedom in American culture. I make nothing new, create nothing: I'm a sort of mad journalist, a journalist without a paid assignment. Twain was obsessed with racism; me, with sexism.

After having traveled through innumerable texts, written texts, texts of stories which people had told or shown me, texts found in myself, *Empire* ended with the hints of a possibility or beginning: the body, the actual flesh, almost wordless, romance, the beginning of a movement from no to yes, from nihilism to myth.

If I had made up this journey, it wouldn't have interested me. Critics have often accused me, and sometimes even my writings, when they distinguish between the two, of being violent, and worse. I make up nothing: I am a reader and take notes on what I read. Whether it's good writing or bad by academic standards doesn't interest me. It never has. What is, simply is as it is. Of course I an interested in learning, in what I don't know, understanding, and if this is the "MAKE IT NEW" that Pound meant, then I subscribe to that tradition.

1989

3.

```
Realism for the
Cause of Future
Revolution
```

1. Realism in Art Language: Simple Descriptions of Some Paintings by Francisco Goya

1. Atropos o El Destino (Atropos The Fates): We Who Are Neither Men Nor Women

Three men are talking. These're the men who cause war. One man has on a Renaissance hat or else has genetically-flawed hair. His right eye is larger than his left so he's smirking, as his shoulders curve inwards. Except for the hat, he's naked. The person facing him is short and has deformed, that is, loopy fingers. All these people are deformed and recognizable.

A man who has light hair, since he's looking into a mirror, is a female. She wears an armless white tee-shirt. The man almost directly in front of her but slightly to her right is ugly. He has ugly monkey lips. Black, greasy hair is dripping down the neck. A classical white toga, the sign of the highest human culture, knowledge, and being-in-the-world, hangs off of his hairy shoulders. His body is unbalanced. These hideous monsters-being-men are controlling the world Our Father Who Art All Men're Created.

They are our fates. They are floating on a white cloud because the world is theirs, those who control this world are above it.

The fourth man: the ape-man is either eating a half-peeled banana or holding a cross. Reality isn't clear.

The ape-man looks down on his territorial holdings: acres after acres of clear fields, streams, running nature. A few trees, you can't tell the difference between tree and tree-shadow or image. All the world could be a reflection.

2. La Cocina de las Brujas (The Witches' Kitchen):

Humans're both dogs and skulls. Both humans and dogs like to eat and feel heat. Skulls just lie there. Human-dogs eat and feel heat in a kitchen. Women control the kitchen or kitsch (men control the den where criminals lurk), but there are no women among the human-dogs or maybe the human-dog whose face is old-approaching-skull is male or female or it no longer matters. Since a broom's sweeping his/her bald pate, the broom-rider must be a witch. The dog-who-stands-like-a-man stares at this broom, and behind him a male skull laughs. What's he laughing at? Another human-dog pisses on the floor because he's a bum pissing in a concrete doorway. These aren't scenes of war: this *is* war.

3. El Aquellare (The Witches' Sabbath):

A big goat is making love to a woman 'cause his paw's on her tit. He wants to fuck this woman. His horns are beautiful. He's horny as hell. Being a beast, he's bigger than all the humans. The woman he wants to fuck, who's holding a baby (all children should die whenever they open their mouths), looks longingly at the beast. In front of her, a crone who has almost dehydrated into a skeleton holds a skeleton up to the monster. He must be their guru or leader. The moon pukes. Another old bitch behind the monster is halfway to being a skeleton. The only foliage in the world occurs not on the ground, but around the monster's horns.

This world is sick. Why? There's no reason.

It's sick because there're monsters in it.

Behind the monster, The Virgin Mary and Her cohorts Who's

palely or politely fading away don't have any expressions 'cause They have no faces 'cause They're pure and religious. The human beings who worship The Beast wear female togas 'cause they or worship is classical, and dead children lie between them.

I see what I see immediately; I don't rethink it. My seeing is as rough or unformed as what I'm seeing. This is *realism*: the unification of my perceiving and what I perceive or a making of a mirror relation between my world and the world of the painting.

One of the humans who's fat and female over her left shoulder holds a stick from which tiny, obviously dead babies hang down. This is her banner. The ground is barren. The hills behind are barren. The sky is barren. The sky is nighttime. Humans are witches.

(4. Imitated by Goya: Pier Leone Ghezzi's The Evening Meal):

A middle-aged mommy has a nose like a pig's and doesn't have a mouth. She doesn't have a mouth because flesh is shutting up her mouth because women don't have language. Instead of having language, women have babies. This baby is uglier than his mommy. It has President Ronald Reagan's eyes, nose, a caricature of a fat slob's mouth, and no body. People bring up kids by training them to stop being. A nose almost as lengthy as a small cock and hair over a head reveals the husband's sensitivity. His mouth is smarmy. He's looking at his child with love. The child is wrapped up like a mummy.

4. Dos Viejos Comiendo Sopa (Two Old People Eating Soup) (this is Goya's copy of the above painting):

A woman who looks like a skull is eating soup. The spoon she's holding faces downward to a wooden bowl as if she's so gaga she can't quite manage to hold it. The hands holding the spoon are big, ugly, and knotty. The face is so thin, you can almost see its bones. Since she almost looks like a man, due to her huge nose, the cloth (shawl?) covering her head is both a female dress and funereal swathing. The difference between life and death in this male/female female is as minimal as the artistry of the brushstrokes: the rough brushstrokes barely indicate what they intend to. Old people're as stupid as newborn children.

The old woman must be fond of her soup, it's probably her only pleasure in life, because she's grinning hard. She's grinning so hard, her grin is the grin of a skull. Big black pupils in her big man's eyes pop out of her head so far, they almost detach themselves from the skull. To her left's a lifeless skull.

This skull is as big as the woman's head, but it's fallen lower than her shoulders. Even though the painting's title says this skull is alive, this skull isn't alive. The expression of the bows of flesh sticking out over its mouthbones is animal. The fingers on its left hand, bones, point toward the old woman's soup bowl. Maybe he wants food. Maybe this is why the female skull's eyes're popping out of her skull: she's happy because she has the bowl of soup. She's not eating it: she doesn't need to eat it. Her spoon is pointing toward the bowl because she owns the food. Ownership is enough. The male skull is lower and deader than her. Ownership, for old people, is everything.

There are no children in this world.

5. Perro Semi-hundido (The Dog):

A dog is sticking its head over a barricade you can't see what the barricade is. The only event that is seen and seeable is the dog's head.

Woof. The only language which is heard and sayable is "Woof."

II. Inset on Language

Language, any language including verbal and visual ones, supposes a community. In the Western world, prior to the end of the eighteenth century, art had a place in the overall society. "Religion and dynasty were the dominant forces that gave art substance over the centuries."[1]

The onset of the French, American, and industrial revolutions allowed or forced artists to question the relations between art and religion and political power. "The Church and the dynasty . . . were no longer there to sponsor art, and the artist was cut off from financial support and from . . . response . . . Now, with the coming of revolution, the artist produced his work in the void. . . He was no longer a man (or woman) whose handiwork was needed by society."[2] Meaning had become a political issue.

The artist has to consider how to make society want his work or accept his nonsense as language, communication. The Black Paintings, some of which I have simply described in the paragraphs above, Goya in the years 1820 through 1823 painted directly on the walls of his farmhouse outside Madrid. These paintings were not on canvases. Goya, who had before always been interested in making money out of his work and was successful at it, didn't want to show these paintings to anyone. He refused to have a language. Why?

What or who is a human who doesn't have language? The Black Paintings are descriptions. They are realistic. I have simply described some of them. They aren't or don't include judgements. I haven't judged them. Are such descriptions communication? What is being communicated? What is being communicated by this "realism"?

Language is that which depends on other language. It's necessarily reactive. An isolated word has no meaning. Art, whether or not it uplifts the spirit, is necessarily dependent on contexts such as socio-economic ones. What can this language be which refuses?

The only reaction against an unbearable society is equally unbearable nonsense.

The Spanish Bourbon government's oppression increased. In 1824, Goya requested a passport to France under the pretext of taking the Plombières' bath waters. In this permanent exile, becoming more and more deaf, in such total isolation, Goya moved in his painting from nihilism (one kind of realism), to painting or visually describing workers. "It was in his work as a painter that Goya discovered his own salvation, and it was in work," the work of negation, "that he found the strongest intimation of the survival of man's dignity."[3] What's this language which describes yet refuses to be reactive, to be only a language which is socially given? It is making.

III. Caravaggio's Realism: Being Itself

1. The Early Sexual World: Self-Portrait As Bacchus (1593–1594?)

A boy is looking at me. What's his look? I see: his flesh's thickness; that, though the muscles are showing in his upper right arm, which is facing me, and in the part of the back below the shoulder blade, the musculature is round and soft; his lips are thick; the nose is blunt and wide. He's sexy. This is his look: he's looking at me sexually. My looking is his identity is his look. This triangular relation (the painting) is sex; desire is the triadic look. This boy is sex.

What's his expression? Sex. What's my look? Sex. This sexual, soft and round, world is (one of) connection.

Since this is a self-portrait, Caravaggio has set up a sexual relation between himself and me.

Since my seeing's (I'm) sexually connected to him, I'm curious who he is. If his identity's sexuality, what's sexuality? Who is the boy?

The leaf-wreath perching on his head indicates he's natural. I'm not positively sure he's looking at/desiring me: his sexuality or naturalness is sly. Sexuality isn't trustworthy.

His hands, near his chin, hold a bunch of grapes. Since he's not looking at these grapes (nature), he wants more than food. Sexual desire must be more than need. He's both weak and strong.

This picture (this looking, this sex) is now about setting up a language. Defining words and their intersimilarities. The world of connectedness.

If this picture's now a setting-up of language, what's art criticism? Looking at him (the boy, the artist) looking at me, mirror on mirror on mirror, is how language works. My verbally describing this visual description is my mirror of/is my being part of this sex, this connected world. This is a living world.

The sheet of a child or a Roman toga falls from his left shoulder under his right arm, downward. His look, sexual desire, which fades as soon as it starts to happen, is ageless. No wonder looking or sexual desire is more complex than slyness: in terms of time, looking or sexual desire is simultaneously eternal and momentary. The boy's physical fragility underlines this momentariness: his muscles, young, about to sink into soppiness; thick flesh is about to become ugly unwantable fat flesh.

The way he's looking at me is mysterious: sexual desire's unlogical or mysterious.

The Gypsy Fortuneteller (1594–1595)

A physically similar young boy who's slightly older in years occupies the whole right half of my visual space. I know he's older because the clothes he's wearing are more sophisticated: a black hat flying a white-and-black feather; an orange velvet jacket (black velvet bands framing its seams) over a frilled white shirt; wide black cloth (as opposed to the first boy's white cotton) flung, seemingly carelessly, over his left shoulder. His right orange-leather-gloved hand, holding the other orange leather glove, rests on his waist, again seemingly carelessly, above the scabbard. He's older than the first boy because he's developed an image; or because he's developed a presentation in the social world he's older.

His face's image is similarly clear. The fullness of the first boy's face, his expression was ambiguous or unknowable. This boy's similarly young full-tending-toward-fat cheek muscles now are knowing: thick lips, whose left ends lift slightly upwards, almost smirk. The nose smells the same smirk. Just as his expression's no longer ambiguous unknowable, so his look's object's no longer questionable. His look, therefore his sexual desire, is clear. He has an identity; sexuality unites with identity. The image is defined, so I'm excluded from this world; I'm excluded from this world so the image is defined. He no longer wants me.

He looks at a young woman. She looks back at him. Her lips, physically like his, rise in the same way his do. Their looks mirror each other; their desires mirror each other, mirror on mirror on mirror on mirror; their looks occur only within the painted space. Their looks form a sphere or enclosure; they have made a world; look reflects look as the spread legs wind around the cock's head and enclose it. The snake bites its own head. When two people look at/fuck each other, they don't see anyone or anything else.

The young woman occupies the full left half of my visual space. The white cloth wrapping around the back of her neatly-parted dark-brown hair then tying under her chin repeats the white of his hat feather. The color of a blouse which hints at being transparent but is actually white, made out of gathers which again almost reveal/hint at revealing a breast, echoes the white of his shirt which peeks out from under his orange velvet jacket. These are the only (almost) pure whites in the painting. Colors, that form, announce relations.

Just as their looks forming a sphere touch each other, so her hands hold his hand. What happens in the upper intellectual world takes place in the lower animal sphere.

Realism

Gypsies're the scum of the earth. No one in her right mind would have anything to do with them. They're (were?) just lower sexual animals. Of course, they're all women and all women being sexual animals're witches. How can these beautiful young aristocratic boy's eyes, his very intellect, his soul, and her scumbeing be one total world? Because the intellectual sphere mirrors and connects to the animal sphere: sexuality is this totality: the looks of these two people, which is my look as I look at them, is a certain definition of sexual desire.

Bacchus (1595–1596?): Realism

A young boy's looking at me. I'm looking at him. This time, though I'm sure it's at me he's looking, his eyes are veiled. His sexuality's questionable. Why questionable?

Again a wreath is sitting on his dark, now abundantly curling locks. Now the leaves are gigantic and huge batches of huge grapes are growing out of his hair; fertility's flowing. Can I handle this boy who obviously wants me, this much fertility and pleasure?

I thought men can only have one orgasm at a time.

His face is more defined than the other two boys' faces: His lips though fat seem thin because they're pressed together. His chest where one tit's actually sticking out is both fuller, rounder, fatter, and has more muscles than the other two boys'. In him male and female physical characteristics have blossomed to their extremes, like the grapes jutting out of his hairs. To a fuller extent than the intellectual and animal spheres within the humans in *The Gypsy Fortune-teller*, here human mirrors plant life. Such abundance, such sexuality is questionable because it's almost unbearable. So the boy's look at me is, beyond sly, complex: his sexuality is this complex. If I accept him, I am this: this nonstagnant always burgeoning almost hideous and comic overgrowth.

This boy isn't beautiful.

Will I be able to accept my sexuality?

A toga like the one the first boy was wearing drapes across his left shoulder (as I'm looking at him). This toga has now become— for even inanimate things burgeon in this overly fertile world—a sheet which falls over the pillows against which he's leaning. His left hand's holding a huge glass of red wine out to me; he's not even bothering to look at me. I can't understand what happens in this world. It's all change. Sexuality or constant change scares me. This sexuality (wine) is that which confuses human understanding.

These changes include all possibilities. Below the glass of red wine, more fruit is bouncing out of a low china bowl. Some of this fruit's decaying. Mold covers some of the spatially lower peaches. Apples are perfectly hard. His left hand's pinky is crooking to the fruit. From this lowest decay and rot up, through his hand, the red wine—this confusion or this totality of all possible possibilities— which he's offering me, up to the head-grapes, from lower to higher: all this is sexuality. This sexuality is unbearable and non-comprehendible not only because it confuses, but also because it incorporates the world. Totality or orgasm is unbearable. This is the world of *The Gypsy Fortuneteller* in all its possible extremes.

His fat right hand's fat second finger crooks around a black velvet bow. The sort of bow a beautiful courtly woman would sport. Does an aristocratic velvet bow, a Roman toga, decaying fruit, and a tiny tit fit in the same look? What identity can this be? How can this be my sexuality, identity? My identity sexuality, if I look here, has to be constantly fluctuating possibilities: things aren't things: fertility. Fertility isn't only bearable: it is (sexuality).

2. Adulthood's Sexuality: Conversion Of St. Paul (1600–1601)

Two figures occupy the space's foreground. One figure is an animal and the other figure is a human. The animal is on top of the human. The animal is slightly bigger than the human.

The animal, a horse, looks almost pensive or melancholy because its eye, the one I can see, is dark and lidded and its head droops downward. As it's (he's? I can't decipher its gender) looking at the human, this animal intends—its right foreleg is raised and poised—to strike downward.

The leg is raised over the human's head. The figure is a male who's lying on his back. Since his head's the part of him closest to me, I can't tell whether his eyes're closed or whether he's looking at the horse's torso's underside. Since his head's turned halfway to my right, he's looking, if his eyes aren't closed, at the horse's eyes. The animal's and the human's looks, as the gypsy's and the aristocratic young man's, form an enclosed sphere: Are they making love?

(The man's eyes probably aren't closed because, as he's lying on his back, his arms, straight out and stiff, rise halfway upwards and to the side. And his legs ((hidden in shadows (the shadow cast by the animal's ass which is closer to him and to me than the animal's face))) ((secretive)) are raised as a woman's are often held when she fucks lying on her back. The man knows what's happening/ about to happen to him: the man's eyes're seeing the horses' eyes. The horse's about to strike the man. This sexuality is dangerous, complex.)

The man's sword lies apart from his body, to his left. Since his face's turned to the right and he's looking that way, he's abandoned his sword. The animal's leg's raised probably over the man's cock. As the animal's and the man's eyes connect, so do their lower parts (again as in the case of the gypsy and the young aristocrat man). Does the man want the horse to kill him? I know the horse's intention. What's the man's? What's sexuality?

The man's eyes're closed therefore he's serene. He more than wants, he's ecstatic or acceptive. Because the horse must be above him.

In the space's background, a man who's old because there're many lines in his face, standing behind the horse's face, holds the face downward. This man is smaller than the other two figures and almost hidden. His clothes, almost unseeable, hint of the peasantry; (the larger man clearly wears warrior drag). The old man looks totally concentratedly down at the horse's head who's looking down at the soldier who's looking ecstatically and unseeingly up at the horse. Human and animal and human—for here acceptance is active—work together; the human social classes—even through violence—work together: as they are in/are the world. Really seeing or accepting this, the soldier, as I see, is ecstatic. The triadic look is sexual desire. This sexuality incorporates more of the world or is more complex than that of *The Gypsy Fortuneteller*.

3. Old Age's Sexuality or the Sexuality from Full Human Experience

The visual space is so dark it's almost black. I have to strain to see. Perhaps my eyes aren't good anymore. Here "realism" is the painter's using his painting as a tool to make a certain perceptual mode, which mirrors and connects to a certain content, occur in me. This is the visual space of uncertainty or old age.

In this blackness there's a beautiful boy. The expression of this beautiful boy's face is clear and strong: eyebrows curve upwards at the beginning of the nose, while eyes look downward to what the left hand's holding; a large Roman nose emphasizes the slightly rigid and melancholy cast of lips, which would otherwise be desirable. Shadows are almost hiding his face's left half. An unsheathed sword in his right hand rests on the uppermost part of his right leg. The precariousness of this sword's position indicates that it's just been used.

David with the Head of Goliath (1609–1610?)

The boy's left hand is holding the second figure: a cut-off head. Since it's cut off, the young boy has just cut it off even though he's looking at it sadly. Since the part of the boy's body which is closest to me is his left hand and the cut-off head is even nearer to me, the boy, though he's not looking at me, is displaying the head to me. A description can't be that which it is describing. This is one of languages' presumptions. Formally, here, Caravaggio's describing or showing. Such description's the opposite of fucking or connecting. As the head's cut off, relations in the world are cut off: the young boy looks at he who doesn't and can't look back at him; I can look at only what I'm shown. Sexuality, disconnected.

Cut-off: The head is a middle-aged-to-old man. Though his features—dark rather than gray and lots rather than scanty hair; a large similarly-colored mustache; a nose physically like the boy's—indicate he's middle-aged; the hair's wildness, the eyes' combinative look of melancholy and contemplation, the open wet mouth's scream agony, the cheek muscles' tenseness indicate a fuller experiential range. The cut-off man has seen everything truly; the dead man whose very being is a scream is the human world. Realism: Caravaggio simultaneously shows me this and makes me/ my perceptual mode be this; (since the cut-off head isn't looking at me but downward and into himself, I'm not being desired: I'm cut off from the sexuality I see). I'm being totally denied. I scream. I live in this world.

The beautiful boy, looking at his own sexuality, has to turn his sexuality or himself into frigidity or an image. The sexual is the political realm. There's no engagement.

1984

Notes
1. Licht, Fred, *Goya and the Origins of the Modern Temper in Art* (New York: Universe Books, 1979). p. 15.
2. Ibid.
3. Ibid., p. 269.

4. Good and Evil in the Work of Nayland Blake

Hansel and Gretel

Famine

There was a great famine in the land. The nation had begun economically disintegrating. A certain father who could no longer provide for his family muttered to his wife, "What is going to become of all of us?"

The mother answered, "Let's take our children to a forest so thick, no one who doesn't know how can escape it, and let's leave them there to die."

"I don't think that's a good idea," said the man.

As if she hadn't stopped talking, the mother replied, "If we don't kill our children, we're all going to die. In a period of famine, two deaths are better than four."

The father wept because he pitied his children. Abandoned children, abandoned only to death.

Innocence

Through the walls, the children could hear their parents planning their deaths.

"We're going to die," said Hansel.

"What's death?" enquired the girl.

"I'll save you."

In order to rescue himself and his sister, Hansel went out into the night. In that night, he stuffed his pockets full of stones. Back in his parents' house, with pockets weighed down by worthless pebbles, he told Gretel that they were saved. "God is protecting us."

The Little Boy Lost

> The little boy lost in the lonely fen,
> Led by the wand'ring light,
> Began to cry, but God ever night,
> Appeard like his father in white.
>
> He kissed the child and by the hand led
> And to his mother brought,
> Who is sorrow pale, thro the lonely dale
> Her little boy weeping sought.

William Blake

Abbreviated Journey into the Forest

"Get up, brats. We're going to the forest."

The brats woke up and their parents accompanied them into the forest.

While they were walking deeper and deeper, the boy secretly dropped stones. In the middle where the forest was so dense nothing could be seen but a chaos of wood and leaves, mother told her children to wait.

The children waited and slid into dream.

When they woke up, there were no parents.

No longer knowing how to leave, where she was, if there were paths, anywhere, parents, home, the girl became hysterical and nauseous. Hansel tried to calm her down by telling her to be patient until the moon gave them some light.

When the moon was so high that bits of its white penetrated through the leaves, Hansel saw his stones and followed them through the forest and out until he and his sister safely reached their home.

The Little Boy Lost
>Father, father, where are you going
>O do not walk so fast.
>Speak father, speak to your little boy
>Or else I shall be lost.
>
>The night was dark no father was there
> The child was wet with dew.
>The mire was deep, and the child did weep
>And away the vapour flew.

William Blake

The Innocents are Free at Last

The country became poorer. The father feared that they were all going to starve.

The mother said, "This time let's take our children into woods so black and pathless, they'll never escape their deaths."

The father loved his children, so he persuaded his wife to give them each a last piece of bread before they were led to death.

The brats were still listening through the walls to everything their parents said. They knew their parents wanted to kill them.

When Hansel tried to leave the house, he learned that his mother had locked the door.

In his innocence Hansel told Gretel that they were safe because God would protect them.

This time on his way through the forest Hansel dropped the only thing he had. Crumbs of his piece of bread. Better to escape from the forest than to eat.

The mother led her children into a part of the forest where they had never been in their lives.

Then the parents ordered them to wait until evening. When the parents would return. Then it was midnight and there would never again be parents.

Infant Joy

> I have no name
> I am but two days old.
> What shall I call thee?
> I happy am
> Joy is my name,
> Sweet joy befall thee!
>
> Pretty joy!
> Sweet joy but two days old.
> Sweet joy I call thee:
> Thou dost smile.
> I sing the while
> Sweet joy befall thee.

William Blake

Eating

Hansel searched for breadcrumbs, but now there was nothing. The birds had eaten everything.

He said to his sister, "We'll find a way out." But there was no way.

Wandered in circles and spirals. The children were hungry. Walked for three days in desolation.

On the next morning, the sun was dazzling away its own color and somewhere in that light a bird was singing. When Hansel and Gretel looked up, the bird started flying. Soon they could see it.

They followed the bird until it stopped in the air and hovered over a house constructed out of food. All the foods about which the children had dreamed.

Hansel stated, "God has saved us."

While Hansel munched on a roof, Gretel licked a window.

Twinkle, twinkle, little bats,
What the hell you nibbling at?
Rats get eaten by big cats
After God has shat.
Up above the world so high
There or in hell you're going to die.

The female voice who sang these words asked why they were destroying her house. "Who are you?"

Hansel and Gretel didn't answer the voice, but went on chomping.

One of the uneaten doors opened and a woman too old to be human hopped out. She told the children that they shouldn't be frightened: she was going to take care of them.

Inside her home, the witch fed Hansel and Gretel German food and then she tucked them into a bed of gigantic mattresses and comforters. Finally the children felt safe enough to dream again.

Witches resemble animals in eye color and smell. They perceive, not by sight, but by smell. This witch, Queen of the Forest, was a cannibal and she preferred children.

Next morning, Witch locked up the boy in an animal restraining cage.

When the girl awoke, she was informed that she was to cook and serve food to her brother so that he would become plump enough for the witch's digestive needs.

While Hansel ate and drank the richest foods in the world, Gretel was fed on burnt matchsticks and diseased pig teeth. (The witch wasn't a feminist.)

Because Gretel was female and also wasn't a feminist, she cried a lot. Her tears made her brother's food so salty, he became fatter.

Every time the Wicked Witch of the West spied Gretel sobbing, she'd make the girl cry harder by describing exactly how her brother was going to feel when the oven's huge flames touched each part of his body. When hot peppers were rubbed into the mucous membranes as they started to split up and ooze liquid.

"If you don't stop bawling," announced the inhuman Queen,

"I'll feed your brother to all the starving children in China." (Witch never read newspapers because she didn't trust reporters.)

Morning, afternoon, and evening the girl did the maid's work. One dawn, while she was doing something too disgusting to name, the witch ordered the child to come to her.

"Come."

Gretel came.

"Climb into that oven."

The child didn't want to climb into the oven because the oven was too hot.

"You stupid brat, that oven isn't hot. That oven is cold. That oven is a virgin oven just like you."

The girl protested that she was scared of fire. Since fire terrified her, she loved to play with matches.

Witch replied that it was no longer cool for women to be weak. Frightened all the time. "C'mon, sister. Get into the fuckin' oven."

Gretel sensed that there was something wrong with this argument.

"If one woman can do it, all women can do it," announced the Queen of the Forest and climbed in.

Gretel quickly shut the door, shoved a refrigerator against it, so the witch burned to death.

There was a smell.

Independence

"C'mon, Hansel. You're free!" She opened the animal cage door. The children were now free to be as they wanted in the world.

Like lovers they held onto each other.

The pebbles had become precious jewels. They ran through the forest until its end and then they walked back home. Their parents were dead.

Interlude

Authors make up stories; no one person invents myths; myths are found, recognized. Myth forms the narrative ground of Pier Paulo Pasolini's films,

... we are taken back ... to the deserted layers of our time which bury our own phantoms.... These are the deserts of Pasolini, which make prehistory the abstract poetic element, the "essence" copresent with our history, the Archean base which reveals an interminable history beneath our own.

Giles Deleuze, Cinema 2

and myth runs through all of Nayland Blake's art.

The realm that is seen when myth is found, the realm of myth and fairytale, identifies human nature. Nayland Blake's art is about what it is to be human.

The Vocabulary of this Myth (Hansel and Gretel and Nayland Blake's Art)

1. Vocabulary: Innocence

Hansel and Gretel are the innocent children. Like Americans seen through European eyes, these children without guilt can and do, without intending bad or evil, destroy (eat) another person's house.

According to both myth and history, the identity of the United States rests upon the following statement from *The Declaration of Independence—The Unanimous Declaration of the Thirteen United States of America:*

> *We hold these truths to be self-evident, that all men are created equal, that they are endowed by their Creator with certain unalienable Rights ... —that to secure these rights, Governments are instituted among Men, deriving their just powers from the consent of the governed,—that whenever any Form of Government becomes destructive of these ends, it is the Right of the People to alter or abolish it ...*

The dream underlying this statement, a statement of and about fundamental human innocence, can be found in the writings of Jean-Jacques Rousseau. A dream or belief that humans are naturally good and in a state of freedom and act for the sake of good. That human evil is caused. That, since humans in a state of freedom do not irreparably violate each other or each other's rights, human society can be noncoercive.

According to Michel Butor, Charles Baudelaire, condemning "America," considered our main mistake to be our belief in and reliance on the natural innocence of men and women. America, Baudelaire argued, was using its material improvements (commodities, etc.) to conceal the catastrophic consequences of "its fundamental error concerning human nature . . . its pretension to virtue, its disregard of the universal and irresistible char-acter of what it calls evil—an error . . . deeply anchored . . . on account of America's initial puritanism."

Nayland Blake's pieces are made out of commodities. All of his art refers to the human body. The body must either be restrained or will become hysterical. Without restraints, Blake's body transforms into a morass of debris, commodities unrelated to meaning. Commodities that at best pretend to mean. Humans or puppets whose eyes are dead. The body, unrestrained, turns into its natural state, chaos. There is no innocence in this world. Here, chaos lurks and lies everywhere; the magic woods is the body itself.

The argument over the innocence of the human is a political as well as an ontological one. Believing in the essential goodness of man (and hopefully woman), our Founding Fathers stated that self-determination, the democratic process, could be the ground of a society. The society did not need to be patriarchal (like the English one we had abandoned) much less totalitarian; and did not need to control, much less restrain, its own populace in order to ensure its own welfare. The current war over censorship is actually a quarrel about the definition of human nature, whether and, if so, how much people need to be controlled. People's actions, dreams, and fantasies. The censorship fight is about the nature of the relationship between humanity and society.

2. Vocabulary: Prison

Humans are social beings; they need a society in order to shield themselves from absolute chaos. If humans are naturally violent or in any way prone to maliciousness or destruction, they must be controlled or restrained by their society if that society is to maintain itself.

The above argument holds if and only if chaos and order are seen to be mutually antagonistic parts of a dualistic system.

In "Hansel and Gretel" the parents represent society; their relation to their children is not one of love, but law. The children begin their journey to adulthood by escaping, then hating their parents.

In Nayland Blake's work, the body finds peace (freedom from chaos) and joy only when restrained, in prison. Since here the restraints are commodities and can be bought by anyone, play occurs only when in the realms of restraint.

3. Vocabulary: Dream Sexuality Art (The Magic Woods)

In the society of law, the society which assumes that humans naturally are at least partially antagonistic to the social welfare, the areas separate from the Logos (always a moral Logos) are those in which all that is human that has been repressed by external and internal means, can express itself. In the society of law, dream, sexuality, fantasy, imagination, and art live outside the Logos.

If the society, still fearing all chaos, suddenly stops marginalizing these realms, of dream, nonprocreative sexuality, and art, and begins viewing these activities as part of its own domain, it will begin trying to control, then censor, then criminalize these phenomena.

According to Descartes, the body is separate from the mind. This conceptual split has today taken the social form of polis (the law) versus art (the body). The law increasingly seems to be regarding art (the body) as the actualization, not quite of chaos, but as the organic incorporation of chaos and death into life, as the violent overcoming of the society-chaos dualism. Those who fear art are trying to make the stink—chaos and death, the spheres of the violent—invisible; trying to banish all that seems ugly and mad (destructions of genres and destructions of limits).

In our society, nonprocreative sexuality, viewed as the road between the cities of the body and those of chaos, is to be banished by the law.

In "Hansel and Gretel," the parents or the law thrust the children into the forest so that they'll die. For the forest is a labyrinth inimical to humans: pathless, unfathomable, and unknowable or chaotic.

In the forest, the only law is magic. The queen of the forest is the witch who doesn't want to control humans, only eat them. Here the children are innocent, not exactly good; hunger, not the desire for good, drives them. The forest is the sphere of the body and of animalism.

The Descartian mind-body split here appears as the society-forest or parent-witch duality.

In Nayland Blake's work, division is represented by the poles of *constraint* and *hysteria*.

In "Hansel and Gretel," the children move out of the labyrinth of the forest, from innocence to self-determination, by killing the witch. Once the witch is dead, they no longer need parents. Parents dead, the children enter society as self-determiners.

This is a fantasy about America. About the dissolution of innocence into the social mold and the simultaneous erasure of evil.

Though Blake's world is composed of the same components, for him evil is indestructible. For there are no parents who can die; there are only commodities: dead-faced puppets and a faceless, unknowable puppeteer. Puppeteers? Like those who control the United States, Blake's parents and Witch cannot be named. Defined. Therefore, cannot be eradicated.

In Blake's art, the body, innocent, must remain caught in the miseries of the restraint-hysteria duality. All of Blake's work forms a portrait of the self mired in the prison of the schizophrenia to which Artaud referred, a schizophrenia which is personal, social and political.

Here there is no catharsis: from this forest or art, there's no escape.

A society defined by such schizophrenia hardly needs to erect exterior prisons.

Speaking for Charles Baudelaire, Butor says:

> What the American appearance seems to promise the bourgeoisie is a futile progress, the establishment of its rule in ever greater comfort and security. What the American reality actually announces, in the mouth of Edgar Allan Poe, is the stubborn persistence of that generous, captivating, indomitable "evil" . . .

4. Vocabulary: Vision

The society censors in order to ensure its own welfare or to destroy evil. If the I (eye) does not censor, it is moving in an amoral realm.

Charles Baudelaire refers to this amoral realm when he discusses several of Edgar Allan Poe's tales. The narrator of "The Tell-Tale Heart" murders an old man only because of the old man's "blue blue eye." In "The Black Cat," the cat's eye "the solitary eye of fire," which caused the narrator to annihilate this animal, remains alive in the dead cat. In "Ligeia," the protagonist realizes that his second wife, whom he has slain, is actually his first, dead wife when he recognizes the "black and wild eyes."

This sight of sight or vision (sight by which the self is known) is art in its highest form. Art according to William Blake.

By his work Nayland Blake forces us to see the puppets' dead eyes. Dead eyes, unable to judge or censor, see clearly, see us clearly. Since such deadness, commodities, cannot judge, we are caught like flies in honey, caught seeing our own unbearableness, when we view Blake's art.

If anything will save us from the labyrinth of ourselves, it is not the seeming destruction of evil, the repression of evil. For repression only creates more of what it purports to repress. What saves us, in and outside of Nayland Blake's work, is this very vision which affirms the undeniability of evil. For the labyrinth is also, and finally, the labyrinth of vision.

According to William Blake, human joy arises from the perception of the infinite which must include that of evil:

> But first that man has a body distinct from his soul is to be expunged: . . . If the doors of perception were cleansed every thing would appear to man as it is, Infinite. For man has closed himself up, till he sees all things thro' narrow chinks of his cavern.

The New Hansel and Gretel in the Magic World: Nayland Blake's Art

"But babies. You've got to admit that it's women, not men, who have babies."

So an artist whom I know, not well, told this story about babies:

He had had this girlfriend, see. Whom he had sent to some rehab center to be rehabbed, or whatever happens to people. Instead of being rehabbed, she had fallen in love with another addict and they had run away from the rehab center.

He, the artist, couldn't stand losing love.

He had had the habit of hanging around Coney Island. Before the girlfriend disappeared. Buying things there. Relics. After love left him, he went back to Coney Island like murderers are supposed to, to the scenes of their crimes.

Boarded-up windows of apartment buildings more decrepit than the old men who work in and work this section of the world. Fleas living on sand.

Tears neither present nor absent 'cause no one cries for junkies.

Slabs of pissed-and-puked-on wood rose out of the sands. Or the smell of dead semen over which water passes, now and then, but never erases. Dead seagulls don't venture to this spot.

It's the dead season so the freaks are ghosts. LEDA, half-swan,

half-woman, no one could guess which half was which. It was all
and it is all dead fish.

As the artist's walking past one of the rotting buildings, the
kind that knows how to stand, an old man, not standing, across
the street says his name.

The artist looks and sees a wiggling finger.

"I've got something for you."

The artist crosses the street to see what the man's got. The kind
of old man that likes little girls.

"Come here." The artist has come here: he's been here before.
Buying. His whole family was touched by cancer.

Down a few streets, there's a sort of building next to an empty
carnival tent. The kind of building that houses those between the
living and the dead. The United States has been here before.

"It's the pride of my collection."

Then down some stairs where there were holes in the wood
that didn't exist, but it was too dark for the artist to see the
holes.

". . . Pride of my collection. A few months ago they declared it
illegal. Declaring everything illegal these days. So I have no use
for it."

Between the living and the dead.

"I'll give it to you for five hundred bucks."

The room below was filled with crap. Refuse of carnivals.
Halves of stripper outfits; green and bleached-blonde wigs; posters
of Madonna and geeks; cigarettes that died in flesh; a dead, stuffed
cockatoo in a huge iron cage swung by a life-size iron woman;
tattooed skin preserved in formaldehyde. The formaldehyde had
seen better days.

In the back was an antique or old table. A large bell jar stood
there. Some sort of thick bubbly fluid filled the jar.

Tiny fingers splayed in the liquid. Some of the fingers were
closing, rigid, as if they wanted a cigarette. Other fingers pointed
to the artist. The huge fish mouth was open.

The artist could smell the dead fish that were outside this room.

He gave the man five hundred dollars.

The room upstairs reminded the artist of one in a museum in his recurring dream.

This part of the natural history museum was filled with aquariums. Inside their cages, fish moved as if alive.

Fish tanks ran from floor to ceiling. Their glass began to shatter. Fish, monsters, and all sorts of debris lay on the floor. Every monster imaginable. The artist, trapped in this museum, felt only horror. The waters began to rise.

The museum was an inescapable labyrinth.

As the artist was walking down the street of dead-fish smells that led to the subway, he looked down at the jar he was carrying and thought that his girlfriend had left him a present.

He, Orpheus.

1990

5.

The World According to Peter Greenaway

1. Anglo-Saxon Culture and Shit

For the European, art is not about product in regard to one or more markets; art is the production of imagination and theory. This actualization helps to define the political and social courses of society.

In our Anglo-Saxon culture, art is increasingly confined to a world of whimsy, an amusing stock market for the rich. There isn't one American artist who has managed to become a spokesperson for even a segment of this culture, whose radical imagination and perceptions haven't been chewed into bits of baby food by the fame factory.

Because we have denied art importance, we have separated its practice from every other form of discourse. Not only the political. Also the religious and the moral. Imagine what education would be if morality were taught according to Flaubert's *Madame Bovary*. The sexual—insofar as the sexual is immoral—is inevitably the province of art today, for many would like to get rid of both.

Throughout his working life, Peter Greenaway, filmmaker, fine artist, and novelist, has situated himself completely in the European culture. If his films are—and are about—any one thing, it is the connections between perception, art, philosophy, mythologies, sexuality, and the political. Perhaps it is for this reason that Greenaway's movies, as he has said, have been hardly noticed in the United States.

In England, since his first major film, *The Draughtsman's Contract* (1982), Greenaway has been accepted as a unique filmmaker; to Greenaway, however, the Europeans are his best audience.

2. Passion

Prior to his latest film, *The Cook, the Thief, His Wife and Her Lover*, Greenaway's films had so carefully balanced visual against philosophical, moral against sexual, documentation against mythology, that they have often seemed dispassionate. In the case of his second film, *Zed and Two Noughts* (1986), disconnected. Whereas a typical Hollywood film depends on a hook, often on a singular story line, Greenaway has never been interested in telling only one tale or in making a point: he has desired to compose a filmic world as complex as the world outside film. And so, to mirror this, the world.

Unlike all of his previous films, *The Cook, the Thief, His Wife & Her Lover*, besides being based on a plot about passion, is passionate. No longer is Greenaway unwilling to make a point, and his story seems surprisingly simple. Whereas his characters, in *Zed and Two Noughts* for example, have been more symbolic than full-fleshed, here they pant as heavily as the story they bear.

All of Greenaway's major films can be identified by a certain style. Visual surfaces that are so lush they almost seem to obscure the subject matter, but never do. For the content itself, a complex of myths and stories, is always too rich to be hidden within sensuous pleasure.

In *The Cook, the Thief, His Wife & Her Lover*, form and visual delight are not independent of content, but work with content for the sake of an almost operatic passion.

3. Margaret Thatcher

When I asked Peter Greenaway why he has suddenly burst into passion, he replied, "Thatcher": Margaret Thatcher and the Thatcherite society, as it's called in England, that she created. Every tendency now, in this society, is to squash quality—to eradicate art, to cut down any endeavor that attempts to exceed itself. Any artwork that involves sexuality is especially suspect. According to Greenaway, this hatred of art and sexuality is linked by Thatcherism, "an incredible vulgarian hypocrisy which slams anyone who makes radical sexual moves . . ."

(There are ways in which Greenaway, though he has thoroughly situated both himself and his work in European culture, is more English than the English. In his films, he has consistently been fascinated with games of sex and power, with speaking indirectly, and with the codes of masochism.)

English society is and always has been firmly defined by class. Prior to Thatcherism, the worst sin any English person could commit was to rise, even to want to rise, above his or her station. Thatcherism has not changed the class system for aristocrats and the poor. Except that, due to measures such as the recently enacted Poll Tax, the poor have been shifted from the gray poverty of the dole to the total devastation of urban America. Thatcher simply made it possible for members of the lower-middle class to rise into upper-middle heaven. Stockbroking and the media. In England, this is radical social change.

The thief in *The Cook, the Thief, His Wife & Her Lover*, exquisitely played by Michael Gambon, is a product of the Thatcherite society. He is pure vulgarity. He has risen "by his bootstraps" from hoodlumism to fashionable clothing and rich food. The decor of the media class. The thief isn't just a vulgar creep: in him, vulgarity—the pure hatred of quality—is evil. Unmitigated evil. No psychology explains his nastiness. There are only political reasons.

For Greenaway: in a society dominated by vulgarity and the God of Money, filmmaking and the making of every art are profoundly political acts.

4. The Quiet Rebel

Though Greenaway's films are always political, they are not so in English terms, for Greenaway does not use a social-realist structure. The English, deeply moralistic, distrust art, as they do all that they cannot explain literally. In all his work—film, painting, and novels—Greenaway has entirely eschewed both painterly naturalism and literary social-realism: both forms dear to his society. As for economics, the funding for his major films has come from European sources. I asked Greenaway if he had always been a rebel in his own culture.

"I had this adolescent dream of being the stereotypical artist in the garret. I was 15, 16. Against parental opposition, I gave up university and began going to a very conventional art school."

That Greenaway had the opportunity to renounce a university education sets his family in the middle classes. Unusual for an Englishman, Greenaway does not announce his class. Nor is he given to discussing personal matters.

"Until I was 16, cinema to me was American or English and basically entertainment—popcorn, Saturday night stuff. Then I saw, completely by accident, my first year at art school, Ingmar Bergman's *The Seventh Seal*. Classic English situation: it was raining so we had to stop cricket. The fat boy of the class said, 'So let's go down to the local porn house.' This guy, who for some reason had to call it 'porn house,' meant *The Seventh Seal*, which he thought was salacious. I suppose it is: there are tits and bums in it. Anyway, the movie was a knockout for me."

From the beginning Greenaway had contrasted the Hollywood and European films. Speaking of *The Seventh Seal*: "I had had no idea that cinema could deal with metaphor, with mythology, with history, with time, and still have a strong, gripping narrative about sex and death. But here it was." Greenaway could be talking about his most recent film. "I went back to see that movie five or six times. I decided I was certainly going to take a great interest in this phenomenon."

From then on, Greenaway saw all the European films he could.

5. The Loner

While in art school, Greenaway equally pursued painting and filmmaking. Not surprisingly, the contemporary English painter who most influenced him was more divorced from the English naturalist tradition than any other English painter at that time. R. V. Kitai.

"He had a big exhibition in the Marlborough gallery in 1963, when I was still in art school," Greenaway said, "and that legitimized for me everything I wanted to do. For he dealt with text and image equally. He was very painterly and yet he had a heavy mixture of politics and sex as subject matter. This I found very exciting." Again, Greenaway could be speaking of his own films.

"Of course," he added, "my interest in Kitai was, you know, '60s. I'm not so sure I particularly like him now."

I love how artists don't lie, but shift whenever they talk about their own work and about those who have influenced them.

Having failed to qualify for the Royal College of Art in film (much to his credit), and after the usual number of miserable, tedious jobs such as selling biscuits (as cookies are called in England), Greenaway "by a series of accidents" ended up in the more than highly respectable British Film Institute (BFI). There he wrote catalog notes for movies that were about to be distributed and, more significantly for him, there he had his chance to view all the American underground movies that the BFI was storing but had never publicly shown.

Greenaway now began making his own movies—16mm black-and-white with stolen stock.

Soon he landed another job, this time at the COI, the Central Office of Information. No longer even disinformation, they say in England. Though this office was once the center for the distribution of propaganda in World War II, it now resembled a geographical mirror of Coleridge's death-in-life. For now, in something named peacetime, the COI sent out "documentaries every week" to explain "the British way of life to the Third World." A leftover from the glories of colonialism.

When I asked Greenaway whether the experimental films that he was making at this time, his earliest films, were influenced by the COI's propaganda films, he answered, "Very much so." For Greenaway, at the moment most influenced by the underground filmmaker Hollis Frampton's movies, was searching for a non-narrative, almost mathematical way to organize filmic material. ". . . propaganda . . . statistics . . . demography . . . it was all ways of organizing material . . . So it was about systems, taxonomies, it was about lists and catalog making." These organizational structures "became very much part of my early language. I made about 300 films, which were all dealing with this sort of material."

Though there was, at this time, a strong avant-garde film scene in London, Greenaway didn't feel that he was part of it. The English avant-garde who "had English experimental film organization in their fist" were either too dogmatic, too absolute in their "Marxist appreciation of filmic theory," or "too domestic."

Again Greenaway found himself outside his own culture, a loner. Now, a productive loner. Someone, unnamed, handed him a thousand pounds to make a new film; the thousand pounds grew into *The Draughtsman's Contract*, Greenaway's first major release.

6. A Different Rebellion Away from Abstraction

The English avant-garde filmmakers and film theorists who clustered around the BFI, such as Peter Wollen and Laura Mulvey, were principally concerned with "an abhorrence of actors . . . with the concept of one person pretending to be someone else. I think," Greenaway added, "there was a deliberate attempt to try to ban actors from filmmaking. Not just stars, the Hollywood star system was a long way from our reach, but even members of the Royal Shakespeare Company . . . Most of the [experimental] films at that time were made without people, a sort of abstract Man Ray type of cinema.

"The other concern was this abhorrence of psychodrama, that wretched American inheritance. That you had to construct plot and character based on cause and events."

These were also Greenaway's main concerns, or dislikes, in those days while he was making his 16mm films. Like Hollis Frampton, he was always searching for universal systems, the alphabet, numerical counting, etc., to structure his material. The search for universal structures led Greenaway into the-making-of-film as its own content and structure. Godard "was going around the world saying that cinema was 24 frames a second and that was truth. So the number 24 suddenly became a cabalistically important number." The processes of filmmaking were becoming filmic material.

Such attention to film—how it is made—partially defines Greenaway's style in all his later films.

At the same time, he began to feel unhappily restricted by these structural determinations and almost imprisoning meditations upon filmmaking. Greenaway realized that he wanted to tell stories.

"And so you did."

"Well, something else happened. John Cage had made a record in the '40s called . . . *Indeterminacy?* . . . for which he collected a hundred tiny narratives, fragmentary fictions. Then he looked for a structure: he would tell each story in exactly one minute. No matter how long the story." A very short story had to be read so slowly that it became incoherent; a long story so fast, equally incoherent. "This incoherence referred back to music, the being of music, just as content or structure about the process of filmmaking refers back to the existence of film. I found this device of an artificial . . . structure on narrative useful, convenient, and pinched it."

More important, Greenaway had found the way to let himself do what he wanted: tell stories. Not only that, but tell many, many stories at once, have a structure that was both narrative and complex. "Tell stories," Greenaway's Englishness popped through, "without embarrassment."

In every major Greenaway film, a multitude of stories and hints of myths form a single structure. In *The Cook, the Thief, His Wife & Her Lover*, this single structure is fablelike, simpler and more direct than in any of his films. But even here, simplicity is not simple: the fable opens, like a fan, to reveal a complexity of other stories and myths.

While Greenaway was moving away from abstract structures into narrational ones, he was moving into story in another way: "I felt isolated, very isolated. For I was fascinated by the early films of Antonioni . . . Antonioni's more about intuition . . . and an unconscious flow of interior dialogue." Greenaway felt that he should be ashamed of his taste. "But I admired them. I didn't quite understand why I admired them.

"One day Peter Sainsbury [the then head of the BFI's production division, who had discovered Greenaway] said: 'All your films are about people speaking to the camera.' I suppose that was part of my documentary background. 'Why don't you get your people to speak to each other?' I thought, well, let's have a go at this. If I can embrace all those things I've previously rejected without losing my cinematic vocabulary . . ."

Finally interested in storytelling and character, and still fascinated by the processes of filmmaking, Greenaway made his first major film, *The Draughtsman's Contract*.

"[For me] the first thing about *The Draughtsman's Contract*," said Greenaway, still a lover of abstract systems, "was that people talked to each other."

7. Emergence of a Form (Content)

Greenaway's new interest in character development and story in no way diminished his more philosophic cinematic preoccupations. *The Draughtsman's Contract* depicts the opposition between seeing and knowing.

" . . . the poor stupid draughtsman, this mixture of arrogance and innocence, gets hooked because he thinks he's drawing what he sees." The draughtsman is destroyed because he believes that what he sees he knows. That what he sees is true. "This clever woman with very strong motives of her own, which have nothing to do with draughtsmanship but rather with inheritance and power and the Married Woman's Property Act, convinces the draughtsman that he's drawing the clues to a savage mystery of which he is the perpetrator. And she convinces him that this is the case, because of his peculiar innocence, and ultimately she brings about his downfall. And his initial downfall is not because he's killed, but because he's blinded. So he loses those very vehicles upon which he's basing his information about the world ... both the shape and the form and the structure of the picture, the film, are relevant to its contents."

Like this stupid draughtsman, Greenaway was trained to be a naturalistic painter. The English school of painting. Both in content and style, he thoroughly rejects naturalism and, here in his most recent film, adopts a kind of Jacobean surrealism. This style is for Greenaway what German Expressionism was for Fritz Lang. Speaking also about his film: "I wanted to draw what I knew. I didn't want to draw what I saw. That was too boring."

Greenaway has always opted for perceptual complexity. But more. The model of seeing mechanistically or learning by rote does not involve questioning, whereas the pursuit of truth does. Greenaway has had to reject the Hollywood film, its simplification of life and refusal to be ambiguous. Irony is not an American mode.

The draughtsman is destroyed because he doesn't ask how knowledge is manufactured in his country. How class and power operate. In this early film, Greenaway opposed seeing and knowing in order to reveal the political realities of his nation.

Content and form in *The Draughtsman's Contract*, acting as mirrors to each other, mix for two purposes: to provide a filmic actuality that is as rich, complex, and ambiguous as what is named "reality," and to question and attack the political realities of England. This will be Greenaway's trademark.

8. Myth

If *The Draughtsman's Contract* is about the opposition between seeing and knowing, Greenaway's next film, *Zed and Two Noughts*, is about twinship, "and therefore about the number two. The left hand must always balance the right hand, mirrors, nostrils, testicles, feet, the two-ness of everything." In this film, physical actuality is the essential mirror of the philosophical, religious, and psychic. We look at pictures of maggots breeding in order to penetrate the mysteries of life and death; seeing rot teaches us about those twins: life and death. Greenaway always turns to the human physical processes, especially digestion and putrification, in order to discover what is truly natural. The real gods. At the conclusion of his new film, this emphasis on physicality multiplied by passion explodes into an image of feminist/political vengeance by means of an act of cannibalism.

"In most cultures," Greenaway continued speaking, "there's this idea that we're born as twins, but must lose the other twin. Therefore we spend most of our lives looking for something which is missing all the time, which is only partially satisfied by pair-bonding." A memory of one of Plato's tales about love. In all of Greenaway's major films, the Greek and Judeo-Christian myths form a narrative substrata. Many of *Zed and Two Nought*'s characters are actually Olympian gods: Castor and Pollux, the twins who arose from an act of bestiality, are the film's two main characters. Venus or the prostitute is one of the two principal women; always two; Juno, fecund, is the other. Mercury guards the gates of the zoo and carries flying wings on his hat. The villain, Pluto, who of course bears a Walt Disney badge in order to identify himself, collects zebras, black-and-white emblems of the judgmental society. Meanwhile Neptune looks after those in the fish house and Jupiter governs the whole zoo.

The mythology of *The Cook, the Thief, His Wife & Her Lover* is Christian: the part of the restaurant where the lovers can fuck is the Garden of Eden. From this garden of many apples, the lovers are expelled into a van full of maggots and rot. This Eden myth is complicated, for as the lovers are moving from life to death, they are saved, for the moment, by death, by the van full of putrifying meat. The Christian myth of transubstantiation. Which itself hints of earlier, pagan myths. The end of Greenaway's film depicts the transformation of violent political vengeance into the ritual of eating and drinking Christ. The transformation of death into life.

This could be precisely what Greenaway is attempting to do in his major films: on the filmic level at least, to change the worst kinds of sexism and other human evil into that which is sacred.

The draughtsman's seeing is not false: it is too simplistic. In all of his films, Greenaway concentrates upon the act of seeing, especially in *Zed and Two Noughts*. In this film, documentation of lower animals breeding and dying, worms and maggots, persuades our eyes by horror and fascination, not only to see but to notice the act of seeing. Greenaway forces us to ask: what are we seeing? What is all this strange documentation about? Seeing is related to myth. Every word or image is related to every other through metaphor, myth, and history and these relations announce and define meaning. Greenaway's complexity is one of myth.

Myth concerns both content and structure. *Zed and Two Noughts* "takes its coloring from the exotic colors of animal life. The toucan's colors, birds of paradise, are reflected in the cinematography which is very bright, very primary, very harsh." On the other hand, Pluto, "the evil spirit, isn't interested in color at all; he's only interested in black-and-white animals . . . the underworld, and he takes as his symbol a zebra . . ." The zebra symbolizes the world of morals, black and white, a simplistic philosophy. The philosophy of the judge. "It also begins with the letter z, very magically, the last letter of the alphabet . . ." It's an animal that "carries its own bars on its back . . . its own cage . . . It's an ideal animal for a zoo."

Just as colors form a structure of precise myth or meaning in *Zed and Two Noughts,* in *The Cook, the Thief, His Wife & Her Lover*, each geographical location is defined by a certain color. Since specific events happen in each location, certain acts are colored in certain ways. The colors, thus, become kin to the emotions and seem to move this passionate, Jacobean world. Here, myth is color; Greenaway is trying to picture, to create, a world in the richest of hues. As opposed to the black-and-white moralism of the "Iron Lady," Margaret Thatcher. A moralism every artist who loves the richness of the physical and the mental must defy.

9. Greenaway

"I was trained as a painter, disciplined as a film editor, have delighted in English literature"—and he has written over ten novels. "All the time I'm aware of continuities. You must remember that I am totally outside the American concern for living off yourself. Therefore, for me, cinema is the philosophy of art. It's about the way man [*sic*] represents himself. I always come back to this."

1990

6.

Red Wings: Concerning Richard Prince's "Spiritual America"

Barger's foresight, drive, and cunning shapes the Hell's Angels into the fearsome gang it is today. Sonny Barger does for the Hell's Angels what Lee Iaccoca does for Chrysler Corp. He converts a sloppy, rudderless organization into a lean, mean no-bullshit company. He trims idiot cavemen from chapter rosters and embarks on an expansionist course that swells the club from 6 chapters in 1965 to 67 in 1987. The assimilation of other motorcycle gangs by the Hell's Angels in the 1970s and 1980s differs only in bloodshed from the corporate takeovers that shake Wall Street.[1]

1. Daddy

The father of the United States of America is the cowboy, one of whose modern-day appearances is the biker. We who live under the sign of myth know that the cowboy is that lonely male individual who, against all odds including Indians, braved all in order not to get rich quick, nor to survive, but to keep on traveling. As Steven Tyler, a contemporary cowboy, announced and keeps on announcing, "Take me to the other side."

Richard Prince begins his *Spiritual America* visually with a picture of daddy. Daddy, on a big horse, is looking off into the faraway which is always invisible.

In the interview which introduces this picture, an interview of course entitled "Extra-ordinary," Prince tells his interviewer, J. G. Ballard, the science-fiction and fiction writer extraordinaire, that he was born in a place in which it is unbearable to the point of being impossible to be. An edge. A zone. The Panama Canal Zone.

Prince is using both content and genre to place us in the realm of myth, of the imaginary which is more true than truth.

He tells Ballard only about his father. There seems to be no mother. At first, this father, whose reality status equals that of Jimi Hendrix, another myth, is a hero: "My father's one of those imaginative criminals who wakes up in the morning and . . . makes a resolution to perform some sort of deviant or antisocial act . . ."[2]

By the end of the interview, daddy is a psychopath.

Here, there is no mommy. Maybe there never has been. Maybe, in the American version of the Virgin Birth according to Prince, it is daddy who immaculately conceives. The artist gives birth. The only woman whom Prince mentions is a stewardess whose nipples daddy cut off during an airflight.

Prince is one mixed-up kid.

Welcome to the Princely American family:

2. Invisible

Sitting opposite the cowboy whose eyes try to pierce the horizon, at the beginning of *Spiritual America*, a woman who has no eyes looks straight forward. Perhaps she is mommy.

Certainly, like Oedipus who tore out his own eyes, like Prince who is trying to cast away his identity and identity in general, she can't be touched. She is mysterious: unknowable, untouchable. This is the model, the classical woman,[3] a woman who looks only and exactly as her beholders want her to look.

She has no need to see, for she is only seen.

Throughout this book or society, the Virgin of the White

Upper-Middle Classes appears again and again, without change, untouched.

Almost all the other women in this book, this America, are biker chicks. They display their breasts openly, for that's how their men want them. Here there are no virgins, only mamas:

> *A mama's jacket reads: "Property of Hell's Angels." She's the one with stretch marks around her mouth . . .*
> *"On some nights, you could have fifteen guys lining up for one girl with quite a few coming back for seconds," (said one biker, not an Angel, who was aptly describing the role of women in his world.) "Some of the girls may have got more than they bargained for, but most of them seemed pretty eager and willing to me."[4]*

The biker chick (Mary Magdalen) and the model (the Virgin Mary): Prince's reiteration of the classic Christian picture of woman. Is Prince simply repeating, as have so many before him, a sexist and patriarchal history?

3. A tail that is lost

This problem is important to me because it is in this place of sexism that I find the power of Prince's art. I shall begin approaching, if not answering, this question by telling a story that has already been told.

This version—a rather political one—of the tale is based on Stephen Pfohl's work in his recent *Death at the Parasite Cafe*.

> *Once upon a time, there was a father; this daddy was King. The King had one or more sons; these sons wanted to be King. They wanted to be King, not in order to change the social structure of the society, the structures of power, and the linked structures of desire, but in order to continue the existing rule of the father.*
> *According to this tale, men's relations to each other are always those of war.*

Now the sons, being members of society, knew the difference between right and wrong: they were moral, decent, and they loved and respected their father as they had been taught. They found themselves in an unbearable contradiction. It is here, in this contradiction, this place, that the story begins. Those who live under the sign of duality cannot maintain contradiction. In order to escape that place which is unbearable or inescapable, the sons who murdered the King in order to gain power—part of which power is the possession of women—had only two choices: either to deny their identities, the selves who had murdered, which no man wants to do because then he gives up power; or to get rid of the corpse. Not only the corpse, but also the memory of the corpse.

In order to maintain the society which will not abide patricide, or for the good of society, the dead King and the death of the King were metamorphosed by means of symbol into the sign of the Living Father.

This image or totem in which power has been invested is untouchable, sacred. Most of all, unable to be interrogated. The unquestionable nature of the totem is Law.

Thus, the purpose of law is to enforce the loss of memory. Each time the sign of the Father repeats itself, as is its nature— for instance in advertisements such as those depicting the Marlboro man—doubling occurs. A double loss of memory: of the paternal slaughter and of the linked adoration and terror in which the original totem was held. This terror-adoration is itself a doubling of the sons' hate-love for the father.

The Law desires a forgetting that human ground originally was named contradiction.

This story, which is just another fiction, can be used to begin to answer my question about sexism and power in Prince's work.

In *Spiritual America*, Prince exhibits three major concerns: identity, women, and repetition or appropriation:

4. IDENTITY (The Male)

Bad jokes lace *Spiritual America*. The type of jokes that fall flatter than a drunk. Almost all these jokes concern identity. The first one runs,

> *I went to see a psychiatrist. He said, "Tell me everything." I did, and now he's doing my act.*
> *Prince is more than anxious, like Oedipus and his eyes, to get rid of his self. All puns intended. Whatever is there in the images in* Spiritual America *to delight the eyes is just glamour, a repetition of advertising tricks.*

In typical Prince fashion, throw-it-away-while-making-it-as-glamorous-as-possible, the notes hidden within the items of the curriculum vitae at the end of the book tell us the most about Prince's view of identity.

Freud said, "The basis of taboo is a forbidden action for which there exists a strong inclination in the unconscious."[5] Prince also believes that identity sits on a sexual or desiring ground. For him, this place is the porn theatre.

But as soon as Prince is there, "He's not sure who he is," because all he finds there are "promises, meaningless marks, parts of the ceremony."[6] Sex has turned into signs of sex and these signs, then, have separated from meaning; they just repeat.

So where can he locate his desire, the basis of identity, in this society which is governed by the Law?

> *His own desires had very little to do with what came from himself because what he put out ... had already been out. His way to make it new was to make it again, and making it again was ... certainly, personally speaking, almost him.*[7]

In Prince's world, there's no stable identity, no maker. Or, if there is any maker, it is only that which is made, the art.

From Rimbaud to Prince.

5. Women

In the story I just told—the history of a tail—there are no women. That is, no women subjects. In the war between men, women are only chattel. Levi-Strauss, according to Stephen Pfohl: ". . . she is faced with the promise of being (passively) given as nothing but a sign between men (at war)."[8]

The biker chick: Biker magazines contain two kinds of pictures of women. Typical of the first, a woman who has a "dynamite" body, silicone breasts and a flat stomach has draped her almost naked self over a Harley-Davidson. She looks sexy as hell: this photo is advertising-glamorous. The second type of picture is a home shot. Badly cropped, blurred, often colorless. A babe who has a bad body (stomach sticking out, natural breasts) is lifting up her often filthy tee-shirt so that her boobs can be seen. This photo is as unsexy as hell.

Prince has taken this second type of photo and restored all possible fetishism. All his babes are hot. Any viewer, not just a biker, would want to touch them.

The model: The woman who's sipping a soft drink isn't displaying the soft drink's name. Advertisements exist for the sake of selling products. For selling the society of products. This one doesn't. This sign's displaying the white phallus straw that's in her mouth and those perfect lips that are sucking that white thickness upward . . .

What Prince is doing here is remembering. He is not transforming women as objects into women as subjects. Rather, he is investing these images of objectified women with all the obsession, fetishism, and confusion which society has deemed wrong, immoral . . . to remember. Prince is remembering that his mother has periods and that he hates her and he loves her. Love plus hate is named desire.

6. Repetition

George Bataille said that all society wants to do is propagate itself. Repeat itself. Like any junkie, maintain.

Law is the basis of society. Identity is the only Law. Because the

Law does not recognize anything other than itself; it cannot recognize any one or thing that is different from it, any radical difference. Law is neither messy nor confused; above all, it is not black.

Prince's work is. He is the Prince of Darkness. Under the guise of glamour, Prince's reiteration invokes anything but the simple repetition of advertising and media images. If the loss of memory —the memory of sexism, sexuality, and paternal murder—has entailed loss of feeling, of affect, Prince's terroristic repetitions regain for his audience the territory of obsession and fetishism.

When I see one of Prince's cowboys, I remember desire (my eyes on my father's cock), absence (daddy doesn't exist for me), and all the other feelings, contradictions, which show radical otherness or difference to me.

The fight against the patriarchal sexist society is the fight against the refusal to allow contradiction, difference, otherness. Hélène Cixous is speaking about the return of memory when she says,

> *When "The Repressed" of their culture and society come back, it is an explosive return, which is absolutely shattering, staggering, overturning, with a force never let loose before.*[9]

Insofar as Richard's work is hot, violent, even disgusting, upsetting, black, and replete with contradiction, he is participating in the struggle against patriarchy.

1992

Notes
1. Yves Lavigne, *Hell's Angels*, New York City: Carol Publishing Group Edition, 1990, p. 33.
2. Richard Prince, *Spiritual America*, New York City: Aperture Foundation, Inc., 1989, p. 10.
3. Talking to me, Prince said that the model is the classical woman.
4. Lavigne, op. cit., pp. 115–116.
5. Sigmund Freud, *Totem and Taboo*, trans. A.A. Brill, New York: Vintage Books, 1918, p. 44.
6. Prince, *Spiritual America*, p. 127.
7. Ibid.

8. Stephen Pfohl, *Death at the Parasite Cafe*, New York City: St. Martin's Press, 1992, p. 167.
9. Hélène Cixous and Catherine Clément, *The Newly Woman*, Manchester, England: Manchester University Press, 1986, p. ix.

7.

On Delany the Magician

On Naming

"I feel the science-fictional enterprise is richer than the enterprise of mundane fiction. It is richer through its extended repertoire of sentences, its consequent greater range of possible incident, and through its more varied field of rhetorical and syntagmic organization. I feel it is richer in much the same way atonal music is richer than tonal, or abstract painting is richer than realistic."

So speaks a man in the book that you are about to read. The man who is the author of the book. Written in 1976, *Trouble on Triton*, by use of the name or genre of sci-fi, carved in literary geography a pathway between novel-writing and poetry.

"I feel the science-fictional enterprise . . ." What is the necessity to name? Why does Delany need to name science-fiction and posit it against other fiction? And isn't there "other fiction" whose territories and strategies are neither minimal nor restricted by the outdated laws and regulations of bourgeois realism?

"Naming is always a metonymic process," Delany writes. That is, a name doesn't tell you what something is so much as it connects the phenomenon/idea to something else. Certainly to culture. In this sense, language is the accumulation of connections where there were no such connections. And so, to Delany, names such as "science-fiction" form a web:

> *All the uses of the words "web," "weave," "net," "matrix," and more, by this circular "etymology," become entrance points into a* textus, *which is ordered from all language functions, and upon which the text itself is embedded.*

It is this web, a web now named Triton, to which I want to introduce you. If you are Dante, I am Virgil: I am taking you down to the underworld. Into the world under, the worlds of language, words, the world in which there is a secret.

There must be a secret hidden in this book or else you wouldn't bother to read it.

Remember: it all comes down. One must go down to see. Down into language. Once upon a time there was a writer; his name was Orpheus. He was and is the only writer in the world because every author is Orpheus. He was searching for love.

For his love. For Eurydice.

Eurydice is secret, a secret. This is how Eurydice became secret: she was walking down by the river, always by water, and a man named Aristaeus tried to rape her. She escaped from him before he got to do anything, but in the process, she stepped on a snake. It bit her; she died.

So Orpheus couldn't see her anymore. Dead, she became secreted, secret. He wouldn't accept her death, death. Every poet is revolutionary. Orpheus started searching for Eurydice, for his secret. For all that was now unknown and, perhaps, unknowable. He journeyed, for he had no choice, into the land of death.

For the poet, the world is word. Words. Not that precisely. Precisely: the world and words fuck each other.

Delany is Orpheus searching for Eurydice by means of words. By going down into words. Into the book. As you read this, you will become Delany/Orpheus.

The book's protagonist, Bron Helstrom, looks for his Eurydice—

who is totally unknown to him. Unknowable? Therein lies the narrative of *Trouble on Triton*: the trajectory from "unknown" to "unknowable." Here, also, is the mystery of the Orpheus myth.

Delany is going to take you to Triton. To a society to which you are a stranger. To all that is other, to the other-world or underworld. Bron Helstrom is also a stranger in this society: you and he will share problems. The book is not named *Triton*, but *Trouble on Triton*.

Every book, remember, is dead until a reader activates it by reading. Every time that you read, you are walking among the dead, and, if you are listening, you just might hear prophecies. Aeneas did. Odysseus did. Listen to Delany, a prophet.

You are about to enter a story or a land in which there is a mystery, a secret, a prophecy about you.

Bron, another appearance of Orpheus, is in the land that is strange to him, in Triton; he's searching for someone to love. Since that means that he's also searching for how to love, he's trying to find himself. Every search for the other, for Eurydice, is also the search for the self. Who, Bron will ask, do I desire? Who can I desire? What does my desire look like? Strange even to himself, Bron learns that he cannot find himself and so he begins to look more widely, more profoundly, and, as you see through his eyes, for he is your guide, you will begin to look. For Eurydice; for yourself. As soon as you find Eurydice, who lies in the center of this masterpiece by Delany, because she is the one who does not lie, *as soon as you see Eurydice's face*, you will know everything.

You shall see desire.

Delany has seen Eurydice's face, for he is also the constructor of Triton; he is the magician. Look at his language. Call it "poetic language." But "poetry" doesn't mean much anymore. This, his, is magic language. It is, as Delany says, not the language of the web so much as the language that makes webs. Delany the author entered into language until language made his desires/questions into a world. The last part of this creation process is you entering the same language by reading until the language shows you you. Delany, a magician.

Eurydice? Where is she? As another woman, Luce Irigaray, has asked: are there women anywhere?

In the utopia/distopia of Triton, women can become men and men, women. In 1976 Delany, magician, was prophesying or creating the San Francisco of 1996. But . . . what of Eurydice by herself?

According to Robert Graves in *The Greek Myths*, Eurydice, whose name means "wide justice," is the serpent-grasping ruler of the underworld. (Remember: she died because a snake bit her as she was running away from Aristaeus.) There in the underworld, she is offered humans who have been sacrificed by injecting them with snake venom.

Eurydice, then, whom Bron/Orpheus cannot find in Triton, in the underworld, becomes Eurydice whom Bron/Orpheus cannot bear to see. She becomes doubly unable-to-be-seen.

Bron, you will learn as you try to see him, is looking for a lover. He has already decided that he isn't homosexual. To find a female lover, he will have to find women, to see them, to understand them, their real sexualities. Increasingly desperate to find and to see love, he will become what he cannot see.

As if it's possible to become what one cannot be/see. For it is possible to change form, to become another form, for Bron to become female with regard to form, but it is not possible to have another history. To really become a woman, Bron must understand patriarchy and sexism, history that he has not experienced.

Orpheus cannot bear to see Eurydice.

As Bron/Orpheus's quest fails, turns in on itself, it changes form. It becomes something other than quest, than story. It becomes Bron/Delany/Orpheus's meditation on gender, desire, and identity. Delany's story refuses to find an ending, to end. Rather it turns on itself like one of the snakes Eurydice handles when she's ruler of the underworld; it becomes a conversation. A conversation, not only about identity, desire, and gender, but also about democracy, liberalism, and otherness. And, perhaps more than anything, a conversation about societies that presume the possibilities of absolute knowledge and those societies whose ways of knowing are those of continuous unending searching and questioning . . .

Enter now into *Trouble on Triton*: enter into a conversation between you and Samuel Delany about the possibilities of being human. By choosing the novel as an area for conversation, Delany is revealing himself as a great humanist.

1996

8.

The Words to Say It

Reading the Lack of the Body: The Writing of the Marquis de Sade

I am using this essay to do two things. To read a short passage from *Philosophy in the Bedroom* by the Marquis de Sade. To read one of his tales.

The more that I write my own novels, the more it seems to me that to write is to read.

1. To write in order to lead the reader into a labyrinth from which the reader cannot emerge without destroying the world.

On January 12th 1794, the Marquis de Sade was taken from the Madelonettes prison to his home so that he could be present at the examination of his papers. The next day, he was transferred to the Carmelite convent on the rue de Vaugirard. Here, he spent a week with six other prisoners, all of whom had fever which was malignant, two of whom died during that week. De Sade was then marched to Saint Lazare, a hostel which had once been a lepers' home and was now a prison.

On July 28 of the same year, Maximilien Robespierre was executed.

In October of the same year, de Sade was again liberated from his jail.

In 1957, a work in two slender volumes entitled *Philosophy In the Bedroom* (La Philosophie Dans le Boudoir),[1] a "Posthumous work of the Author of *Justine*,"[2] appeared in London.

The Purpose of Fiction

Philosophy In the Bedroom consists of seven dialogues. Two of the four speakers are typical Sadean monsters, a Madame de Saint-Ange who in twelve years of marriage has slept with 12,000 men[3] and Dolmancé, "the most corrupt and dangerous of men." The third, the Chevalier de Mirvel, not quite as libertine as his sister, Madame de Saint-Ange, but then he is a man who has heterosexual leanings, nonetheless, willingly assists the others in their seduction of the fourth speaker, a fifteen-year-old virgin, Eugénie de Mistival. *Seduction*, as in *corruption*. In the Sadean universe, these two acts are equivalent.

By the end of the seventh dialogue, Eugénie had been seduced. In fact it took no time at all, ten or twelve pages, for the scoundrelly adults to rob the poor child of her virginity, Sade-style, in the ass. But true virginity, for the Marquis, is not physical. It takes the monsters of corruption more than 150 more pages to teach Eugénie that she can do whatever she pleases: fuck and get fucked in every possible way, blaspheme God, ... disobey, fuck and sew up her mother's cunt to ensure that her mother will no longer interfere in Eugénie's affairs.

The surface purpose, then, of the long and often tedious arguments that occupy most of *Philosophy* is the corruption of Eugénie. De Sade's deeper purpose in penning these dialogues could not have been the seduction of a fictional fifteen-year-old. Of a virgin who despises virginity and, even more, her mother—always a sign in the Sadean universe of a propensity for freedom.

Most probably Eugénie was a fictional representation of de Sade's sister-in-law, Lady Anne Prospère de Launay. Though married to the older sister, de Sade had fallen violently in love with Anne; she returned his passion. De Sade's mother-in-law, Lady Montreuil, angered at least by the sexual delights of these two, did all that she could and succeeded in procuring de Sade's legal confinement.

If the authorial purpose in the writing of *Philosophy* was revenge, if de Sade's purpose was to sew together, fictionally, his mother-in-law's lips, all of her lips, it was poor revenge at best. In 1781, Mademoiselle de Launay died unmarried. De Sade had not seen her since his imprisonment in Vincennes. The Marquis did experience a strange revenge against his mother-in-law. In August 1793, out of jail, he wrote, "I am broken, done in, spitting blood. I told you I was président of my section; my tenure has been so stormy that I am exhausted. (. . .) During my presidency I had the Montreuils put on the liste épuratoire (for pardon). If I said a word they were lost. I kept my peace. I have had my revenge."[4]

For a man as furious as de Sade, writing must be more than fictional revenge. Writing must break through the representational or fictional mirror and be equal in force to the horror experienced in daily life. Certainly the dialogues of *Philosophy* are seductions. But seductions of whom? Why did de Sade, born into the upper classes and then pent up in prisons not directly of his own making, want to use writing only to seduce?

Women in the World of Men

Towards the end of the third dialogue in *Philosophy In the Bedroom*, Eugénie, no longer a virgin in a number of ways, admits to her female teacher that the most "certain impulse" in her heart, note that she does not say "deepest," is to kill her mother. Eugénie is admitting to nothing: almost as soon as she met Dolmancé and Madame de Saint-Ange, she stated, still virginal, that she loathed her mother. Dolmancé and Saint-Ange had no liking for theirs. Now, the girl and the woman talk about the position of women in society.

Dolmancé interrupts with the man's point-of-view. He informs his pupil that a woman in this society has but two choices: to whore or to wife.

Due to her class background, Eugénie is not destined for prostitution, Dolmancé continues, so she must consider her future position as a wife. If she is to survive, a wife must serve her husband. Husbands know three sexual positions: "sodomy, sacrilegious fancies, and penchants to cruelty." The wife's positions with regard to her husband's desires are gentleness, compliancy, and agreeableness.

Dolmancé's opinion is that, in this society, women must serve men in order to survive. No wonder that the women who want more than this, who want their freedom, hate their mothers. In de Sade's texts, mothers are prudes, haters of their own bodies, and religious fanatics, for they are obedient to the tenets of a patriarchal society. The daughter who does not reject her mother interiorizes prison.

The daughter who rejects her mother, such as Madame de Saint-Ange, such as Eugénie, finds herself in an unbearable position. In the patriarchal society, for women freedom is untenable. As regards Eugénie's freedom to kill her mother, Dolmancé argues, she is free to do this, she is free to do any act, as long as she employs guile and deceit.

A woman who lives in a patriarchal society can have power, control, and pleasure only when she is hypocritical and deceitful. With this statement of Dolmancé's, de Sade has erected, or laid down, once more, the foundations of the labyrinth of logic.

Now, the maze begins to be built. Dolmancé continues: Women are free to choose to act like men. Women can "transform (. . .) themselves into men by choosing to engage in sodomy." In sodomy, the most delicious position is the passive one. In other words, a woman can know freedom by choosing to counterfeit a man who selects the bottom power position. Here is one example of deceit.

"(. . .) 'Tis a good idea," Dolmancé continues to instruct his student in her search for power and pleasure, "to have the breach open always (. . .)." For her to remain an open hole.

Dolmancé may be seducing the seduced; that is not the purpose of this argument. Clearly de Sade is not. In this and other dialogues, de Sade is blindfolding his reader. The reader believes that she or he knows how to think, how to think logically, how to know; the reader believes that she or he can know. The cogito. De Sade is leading this naive reader into the loss of belief in the capability of such knowledge, into the loss of sense. And leaving the reader in her or his lost-ness.

It is here in this text that de Sade abandons the male gaze.

Abortion and Logic

A woman talks to a woman about the position of women in a male-determined society; Madame de Saint-Ange and Eugénie continue the discussion of women, freedom, and sodomy. A woman invariably gives up any hope of freedom, mentions the older woman, as soon as she has a child. A woman who wants to be free, above all, must avoid pregnancy.

The discussion about female identity in society narrows down to the problem of abortion. Women's freedom, Saint-Ange says, depends upon her ability to stop pregnancy.

De Sade argues in order to seduce.

These days, a typical pro-choice liberal will say that women must have the right and, therefore, the opportunity to control their own bodies and make their own moral choices. Eugénie sidesteps all liberalism; she asks whether it is morally permissible to abort a child who is just about to be born.

Madame de Saint-Ange picks up this ball and runs home. Home, for de Sade, is located in hell. She replies that abortion is equivalent to murder and that every woman has the right to murder her own child. "Were it in the world, we should have the right to destroy it."

Dolmancé bursts into the female gaze, but does not bust it up, by bringing up the subject of God: That "right is natural (. . .) it is incontestable." Only a belief in God, rather than in Nature, could lead a human to value an embryo more than herself.

Note Dolmancé's mention of or call to Nature. In the patriarchal society, there are no women; there are only victims and male substitutes. And men. Nature is female because, as is the case with women, she does not exist. She does not have existence apart from that gaze which is always male or male-defined. Luce Irigaray on the subject of the possible nature of Nature within the patriarchal structure: "Of course what matters is not the existence of an object—as such it is indifferent—but the simple effect of a representation upon the subject, its reflection, that is, in the imagination of a man."[5]

De Sade is not presenting nor has he any interest in presenting a pro-choice argument. He has as little interest in abortion as he has in Nature, in the nature of Nature. In the nature of women. De Sade is talking about abortion in order to seduce us, his readers, into the labyrinth where nothing matters because, there, nothing can matter. Nothing can mean anything, for all is confusion. De Sade is a patriarch who hates patriarchy and has nowhere else to go. And, jail-rat that he is, raging in his cage or maze, he uses text to overthrow our virginities, virginities not born from the body but from the logos; he seduces us through writing into overthrowing our very Cartesian selves. Neither male nor female seem to be left . . .

II. Reading a tale by De Sade: Writing or reading whose only purpose is to destroy itself

"(. . .) The traces of my tomb will disappear from the surface of the earth as I hope my memory will vanish from the memory of men."[6]

—The Marquis de Sade

The Body

In 1778, de Sade projected a collection of stories entitled *Contes et Fabliaux de Dixhuitième Siècle Par un Troubadour Provençal.* The book would consist of thirty stories; tragedy would alternate with comedy.

The collection never appeared. In 1800, eleven of the tragic and dramatic tales were published in four small volumes under the title of *Les Crimes de l'Amour.*

The Garden of Logos

One of these crimes, named *Florville and Courval, or the Works of Fate*, begins as a fairy tale: good exists; evil exists; good is the opposite of evil. A certain Monsieur de Courval is a good man because he is sexually strict or pure. His former wife was a bad woman because she liked to have sex and was libertine.

Within the fairy tale genre lie the assumptions that its readers, if not the characters within the fiction, are capable of making moral distinctions and that morality is dualistic.

This fairy tale world borders on being mechanical: M. de Courval is good; therefore he is seeking out the good; therefore he is searching for a good wife. (A new wife.) Through the help of a friend, he finds a wife-candidate who seems to qualify as good. Now the marriage or the end of the fairy tale should take place, but it doesn't.

The site of the fairy tale turns into that of the law court. The language of the fairy tale turns into that of the law court. Behind every fairy tale lies the law. Since the wife-candidate is an orphan, her class is unknown. Therefore, her moral status and, so, her identity is unclear.

M. de Courval must decide whether or not the woman is good enough to marry. Since he is rich, male, and nineteen years older than her, he possesses all the attributes of a judge: he ought to be able to judge her moral worth. If she is judged good, the law court will turn into the place of marriage. If not, the characters and the reader will find themselves in the site of tragedy.

The Woman's Tale/Her Version of the Garden of Logos

The wife-candidate, a certain Mademoiselle Florville, announces that she will tell a tale, her tale, so that the older, rich man will be able to judge her properly. She adds that she is presenting Courval with this autobiography to convince him not to marry her. In this morally-defined society, her desire is irrational; here is a hole, the first in the mechanistic movement of the ex-fairy tale, of the morality-determined cause-and-effect. In de Sade's texts, every lapse of logic or hole announces the site of a labyrinth. Every labyrinth is a machine whose purpose is to unveil chaos.

Remember: in de Sade's texts, stories exist for the purpose of seduction.

De Sade constructs his labyrinths out of mirrors. Mademoiselle de Florville's story, in its beginnings, mirrors the narrative in which it is located. Just as there were two poles, good and evil, or the husband and his ex-wife, in the outside story, here the reader, through Mademoiselle de Florville, meets Madame de Lérince whose soul is beautiful (and, presumably, whose body does not exist) and Madame de Verquin in whom "frivolity, the taste of pleasure, and independence" reign supreme. Both these women are kin to M. de Saint-Prât, Florville's substitute father. In the larger tale, since Florville was an orphan, she was situated between the poles of good and evil; in this story within a story, the two older women fight for control over the site of Florville's body.

This story within a story begins with Florville, the untouched body. So that no one will suspect him in all his goodness of harbouring secret incestuous intentions, her guardian, M. de Saint-Prât, sends her off to his sister, Madame de Verquin.

His act, whose intention seems good, leads to evil. In its beginnings, the female's garden of logos is morally muddy. Madame de Verquin introduces Florville to her "handiwork," a youth named Senneval. Senneval proceeds to seduce the young girl, impregnate her, refuse to marry her, abandon her. Eugénie, now quite muddied, bears a son whom Senneval removes from her.

Has Eugénie become evil? Not yet, judges her substitute-father, as M. de Courval will judge, when Eugénie returns to him. He tries to show her that she can still return to the good or proper path of the garden: "Happiness," declares M. de Saint-Prât, "is to be found solely in the exercise of virtue (. . .). All the apostles of crime are but miserable, desperate creatures." He adds that society is vitally interested in seeing good multiply and flourish.

Georges Bataille in his *Literature and Evil*, whose sixth essay is devoted to the work of de Sade, replies that society's only good is its own survival, that "society is governed by its will to survive."[7]

The fight between good and evil for the body of Florville is in full sway. In order to ensure that she becomes good, M. de Saint-Prât now sends her off to Madame de Lérince. At the same time, "a secret feeling" which is drawing her "ineluctably toward the site of so many past pleasures" keeps the young mother in touch with Madame de Verquin.

Once penetrated, the body or garden cannot forget the pleasure that stemmed from its penetration.

That garden whose paths are still clearly labeled *good* and *evil* though they touch and cross each other will now become a maze. Knowledge with regard to the ability to make moral distinctions, thus the capability for judgement, disappears. A catastrophe, "a tale so cruel and bitter it breaks my heart" takes place. Madame de Léringe, this good woman, introduces Florville who is now 34 years old, no longer innocent, to a boy half her age. The Chevalier de Saint-Ange. A dangerous situation for a woman. His origins, like Florville's, are unknown; unknown, the state of his morality.

The second narrative mirror: When Saint-Ange is in the act of raping Florville, she believes that her sexual past with Senneval is repeating itself. In order to shatter the mirror *whose name is abandonment and pain*, she kills this lover/rapist with a pair of scissors. As soon as Florville recognises that she has murdered the boy, she cries, "Oh you! Whose only crime was to love me overmuch (. . .)."

This second narrative mirror does not reiterate and aid sight or understanding: it only blurs and confuses. Florville's moral status is now not confused, but unfathomable. Was she right or wrong to kill? Was Saint-Ange driven by passion or by unjustifiable aggression and violence? Why did she murder Saint-Ange? Was she motivated by her memory of the past, by her fear of again yielding to sexual desire? Did she murder because she too blindly obeyed the moral dictates of her society, because she too deeply feared that she might not be good? In this case of rape and of murder, who is good and who is evil? In this case, what is the good and of what does evil consist?

What is certain is that with the end of the first half of Florville's autobiography, de Sade fully abandons the languages of the fairy tale and of the cold, precise narrative of the law court. The formal verbal garden of morality whose arrangement is that of the logos has decayed; all that is left is the wilderness, almost the chaos and violence, of passion. Florville began to speak this language, this language whose narrative irrationality guides, when she admitted that something in her, something "secret," unfathomable or unspeakable, was attracting her to Madame de Verquin, to the home of Madame de Verquin. As soon as she has scissored Saint-Ange, she speaks nothing but this language: "(. . .) My feelings for you were perhaps far superior to those of the tender love which burned in your heart." Florville confesses to the corpse of her rapist who or which is also the corpse of her moral worth.

The first half of the woman's story ends in this: In confusion crossing over into chaos. In the overthrow of moral distinctions. Such was Florville's purpose when she began to talk, to tell her tale, to her judge.

Interlude

Yet Courval has not been overthrown. Not yet overthrown to himself. He does not yet sit in horror: he still believes that he can judge another person. A woman. He informs Florville, with a return to the language of the law court, that because the murder was not premeditated, she is innocent of that murder, therefore he wants to marry her.

The Destruction, Through the Female Gaze, of the Male World

Florville may have caused the garden of logos to wither away, but since she has not destroyed Courval, her judge or husband-to-be, she continues her tale.

Remember: in de Sade's texts, stories exist for the purpose of seduction.

M. de Courval has just informed Florville that her rape by and murder of Saint-Ange does not matter; now, within this story-within-a-story, M. de Saint-Prât and Madame de Lérince who are also good tell Florville the same thing. They hide her murder from the world.

This third narrative mirror in which the good aid and abet a murderer announces the reality of dream.

The language of passion; now, narrative controlled by dream. Who needs Freud when de Sade's around? The world of logos is in the process of dying; now there is dream; soon death will reign through the garden of identic terror.

Then, there shall be no more judgment, no more the law courts of the world.

Florville dreams a dream in which Senneval shows her two corpses. One is the corpse of the past, male. It or he is Saint-Ange. The second is the corpse of the future, female. She is strange, as yet unnamed.

After the dream is over, the world of death begins. Death upon death will litter the remainder of Florville's autobiography, of her seduction of her listener, of her destruction of his male gaze.

The death of Madame de Verquin. Good and evil have reversed themselves. In this world. The evil woman dies beautifully. Since she lived through and for the body, since she accepted materiality and its laws, the swing and sway of change and of chance, Madame de Verquin accepts her imminent death and dies with "courage and reason." For she does not attempt to cling to possessing, to use possessions to rigidify identity: she wills all of her possessions to be flung, after her death, to whomever according to the dictates of the lottery.

Second, the death of a strange and older woman. Florville is responsible for sealing this "woman's doom." Seemingly by chance, for Florville does not recognise the stranger, for Florville understands none of what she sees nor what is happening. This is the realm, beyond good and evil, of chance.

Before she is executed thanks to the words but not the will of the narrator, the stranger tells Florville that she had dreamed a dream about Florville before she ever met Florville. Dreams are true in the realm beyond good and evil. The stranger dreamed that Florville was with her son and a scaffold. Now, we, the readers, understand none of what we are reading.

The third female death is of Madame de Lérince. Back in the world where evil is good, and good, evil, this most saintly of women dies miserably, stuffed like a potato with remorse and regret. "Madame de Lérince's fears are virtue's anxiety and concern." The universe of judgment and of the law is not only the one in which good is evil, evil, good, but is the place where virtue creates fear. Fear, the illusion that gives birth to all other illusions. Fear of the past returning and the fear of not being virtuous once drove Florville to murder Saint-Ange with a sewing tool.

Florville's autobiography ends here, in death.

Interlude

Yet Corval is still alive and still believes that he can judge Florville and thus marry her.

Destruction, by the Male Gaze, of the World of Men: Oedipus Inverted

As in *Oedipus Rex*, a stranger now enters and tells his tale:

He identifies himself as one of the two children born to Courval and his first wife, the son who was as debauched as his mother. Estranged from his father, he is now strange to his father.

He next identifies himself as the Senneval who seduced Florville, then spirited away the male fruit of that seduction.

That male fruit, when he grew up, raped and was murdered by his own mother, Florville. Senneval further explains that the older woman whom Florville had not recognised and whom Florville's testimony had condemned to execution was Courval's first wife. Senneval's younger sister did not die as Courval had believed; her name is Florville.

The stranger has not told his tale to seduce Florville, but rather to instruct her who she is. For the first time in her life, she is no longer an orphan. For the first time in her life, she knows that she did not will yet caused her mother's death, slept with her brother, murdered her brother's and her son, and might marry her father. For the first time in her life, Florville has been given an identity card into the world of human and the name on that identity card is *unbearable*.

The fourth narrative mirror: As the stranger was once strange to his listeners, Florville was strange to herself. No longer strange to herself, her knowledge, which is always self-knowledge, is not bearable. In the same way, de Sade was once strange to us, his readers. De Sade, the monster. Strangers and monsters: outsiders. As the stranger told Florville his tale and strangeness was disappeared into the chaos of self-knowledge, so de Sade was telling his tale and now is no longer strange. "For I am de Sade; I am that monster."

Whose name is human.

The Body, Disappeared

Oedipus was able to deal with his knowledge of the self whose logos is chaos by casting out his own eyes. *Casting* as in *castrating*. Florville cannot castrate herself: at the end of "Courval and Florville" when there are no tales left to tell, Florville must commit suicide and does. This is de Sade's tale: the nontale, the tale that does not exist. De Sade, also masochistic, bound up, pent and spent in prison, had no tale left and nowhere to go.

For Florville and for de Sade, there is only the world in which this tale began, the world dominated by men, the world of male language, prison.

Regard the Oedipal myth: The Law of the State forbids, above all, the murder of its King. At the same time, since no human can be immortal, the real survival of the state depends upon that very death and the replacement of the King. The Law protects, by repressing, and all repression is also the repression of knowing, the division between the symbol, the immortal Head, and the symbolised, the human who, though king, is himself subject to the laws of materiality, especially of sexuality and of death.

As soon as Oedipus answers the Sphinx's question correctly, he has access to the symbolised or the verboten: to the body and sexuality of his mother. The Law is not patriarchal because it denies the existence, even the power, of women: after all, every King has

His Queen. The Law is patriarchal because it denies the bodies, the sexualities of women. In patriarchy, there is no menstrual blood.

De Sade has nowhere to go because, for him, there are no actual women. In his texts, women are either victims or substitute-men. Hating the society based on centralised power (the immortal King), de Sade most often chose to see through the female gaze, but this female gaze is still the gaze, that act of consciousness that must dominate, therefore define, all it sees. The gaze—which, though seemingly female, is always male—is that sight whose visual correspondent is the mirror. In the mirror, one only sees oneself. Since there are no women, women with bodies, for de Sade, he cannot escape the labyrinth of mirrors and become all that the law has repressed.

When the mirrors break, to *see* is *to become*.

De Sade did not cast out his eyes (castrate himself). Rather, he shattered mirror after mirror; behind every mirror stood another mirror; behind all mirrors, nothingness sits. De Sade wrote in order to seduce us, by means of his labyrinths of mirrors, into nothingness.

De Sade wanted to show or to teach us who we are; he wanted for us to learn to want to not exist. This is nothingness. He wanted his fictional structures to be mirrors of the world or that horror from which, for him, there was no escape: "(. . .) The traces of my tomb will disappear from the surface of the earth as I hope my memory will vanish from the memory of men."[8]

De Sade, born a patriarch, understood patriarchy and raged against the walls of that labyrinth.

Notes
1. Since I am reading from the English translation, I shall refer to texts by their standard English titles.
2. Gilbert Lély, *The Marquis de Sade, A Biography*, trans. by Alec Brown (New York: Grove Press, 1962), p. 391.
3. Note de Sade's realistic tendencies.
4. Letter from de Sade to Gaufridy, quoted in Geoffrey Gorer, *The Life and Ideas of the Marquis de Sade* (London: Panther Books, 1964), p. 52.

5. Luce Irigaray, *Speculum of the Other Woman*, trans. by Gillian C. Gill (New York: Cornell University Press, 1985), p. 207.
6. De Sade quoted by Apollinaire quoted by Georges Bataille in his *Literature and Evil*, trans. by Alastair Hamilton (New York: Urizen Books, 1973), p. 89.
7. Bataille, p. 6.
8. Bataille, p. 89.

9. Critical Languages

First of all, my thanks to Allen S. Weiss whose book *The Aesthetics of Excess* I have learned from and used, and to Steven Shaviro for his passionate *Passion & Excess*. And to George Bataille and the other members of the group Acéphale.

Introduction

When the Divine Marquis, as some have named him, in his *Philosophy in the Bedroom* has his characters "socratize," he is not only referring to Mr. Socrates. He also is pointing to his society's conflation of "mouth" and "anus" ("philosophize" and "sodomize"): a conflation that has, perhaps, been one result of the Descartian mind-body split, that model of human identity.

The current antisodomy law in Georgia reminds us of this equation of mouth and anus in its definition of *sodomy:* "A person commits the offense of sodomy when he performs or submits to any sexual act involving the sex organ of one person and the mouth of anus of another."

On the one hand, this society's confusion between or equating of the mouth and anus reveals a certain truth about its law-making sector: That they, or we, all the judges, make laws, render absolute and often life-destroying judgments prior to the act of under-standing, even the understanding of our own language. On the other hand, this society's equation of mouth and anus has as one of its sub-clauses the following statement: if acts involving the anus, when sexual, are crimes, so are acts of the mouth, expressions, that refer to sex and sexuality.

Art and artist have always been marginal to this polis, the political body. Right now, our government is increasingly attacking acts of the mouth, written and oral speech, which pertain to those parts of the body not ruled by the logos, and acts of speech occurring in other media, visual, theatrical, etc. Once only marginalized, art and artists are slowly becoming criminalized by a government whose real heads are just heads, invisible, without bodies.

It is imperative to return to the body, to return the body. I am going to talk about language, the language of art criticism, but only insofar as that language relates to and occurs in the whole body.

Personal Language Personal History

I'm not an art critic. That is, excuse these remnants of Marxism (I am told that Marxism is an outdated model), I have not and do not earn my living by writing art criticism. In my twenties and early thirties when I lived and wrote in New York City, I was part of the art world. Primarily because my friends were artists. Musicians, painters, performance artists, filmmakers, dancers, anything but writers. We hung out together, shared problems and misery, usually poverty, though I'm not sure poverty's shareable, fucked each other, and worked together. Later on, I wrote some articles for ARTFORUM and a few other publications: all of these articles rose, first, out of friendship. Friendship and an inclination for what I call *joy*.

I actually grew up in New York City, a rarity for those in the art world who lived in the city, spent my college years in Boston and

California, and returned to New York for all the early adult years except for two escapes to San Francisco. Even prior to college I was an art-world baby. When I was fourteen years old, I would sneak out of my high school in order to hang around with downtown avant-garde filmmakers and painters who were probably far more fascinated by my schoolgirl uniform than by any other aspect of whatever's called "me." I remember, when I was fifteen, Jack Smith telling me that what he most wanted to do was to build a huge dome somewhere in North Africa. Whoever entered this dome would tell Jack his or her dreams and instantaneously Jack would make a movie of this dream or series of dreams. Movies would be shown twenty-four hours a day.

Most of all, I remember being taught that it's not an art work's content, surface content, that matters, but the process of making art. That only process matters.

After that, I was taught by the Conceptualists that all that matters, in art, in the making of art, is the intention, intentionality. To use Zen language: one should not mistake the finger that points at the moon for the moon. That all that does not concern intention is simply prettiness; that prettiness is, above all, despicable.

These were the golden cowboy days of art. Unfortunately or fortunately, certainly by some act of fortune, I'm female.

I learned in the New York City art world many other things. That every phenomenon, every act is a text and all texts refer to all other texts. Meaning is a network, not a centralized icon. Most of all, I learned that it is art that matters, the making of art that gives value to my life and that I'm allowed, indeed I *must* do whatever I have to do, to make art.

I thought, in those golden days when poverty was noble and the United States was rich, art is our way, our true Western religion.

Six years ago I started to live in England; except for brief working tours, I didn't return to the United States and to New York City until January of this year.

England, as I'm sure you know, is a society defined, even dominated, by class. Whereas money generally orchestrates social and political differentiation in the United States, in England differences of birth define human possibility in almost every way.

Specifically regarding class in England: approximately 1½% of the English population has gone to Oxford or Cambridge, the two top universities. This 1½% comes mainly from the upper and upper-middle classes. Class, as I have mentioned, is determined, not by wealth, but by birth. The 1½% then proceeds to occupy the seats in Parliament, the top jobs in media—in short, to organize and control the polis politically, socially, and culturally.

The closest friendships of those who attended Oxford and Cambridge were formed at university and shape lives, including business lives, after university.

Looking for an art community similar to the one I had left in New York City, in England I found an art world, if not composed, then certainly defined by the upper-middle class. In the United States, art is not necessarily linked to education and the quality of higher education, though increasingly tied to money, has little to with class. Whereas in England, higher or fine art, education, and class form a trinity. The English who come from the lower classes and want to make art usually position themselves in the fields of fashion, graphic design, and music, particularly rock'n'roll.

Class war runs through, almost runs, English life. Football violence and the more-than-occasional kneecapping of police that is increasingly taking place at the edges of the large urban centers are occasions in a society at war with itself: the lower and lower-middle classes, unable to fight directly against the subservience they've been taught from birth and by history, are battling in the only ways they can, by means of acts of seemingly meaningless and unjustifiable violence.

When in New York City, art (to me) had resembled an angel miraculously living amid the greed and zombielike behaviors of those outside the art world, the faceless business-suits who crowded into Wall Street every morning. In England, the political environment in which art occurred inevitably defined art, made art and the art world resemble, become another game played by the upper and upper-middle classes for their own amusements.

(By *art*, I mean that which is accepted as art by the gallery system, the art buyers, the art magazines, etc.)

In this context of class war, I began to question art, what art can be in such a world. I then started to question all the precepts, the definitions of, the clichés of art that I had imbibed as an art child. What were and are the political realities surrounding Conceptualism? Is it true, or rather, is it right, proper, for an artist to do anything in order to make art? And what of race? Why was the art world in New York, a city whose population is now dominated by nonwhite groups, almost entirely white?

Then I began to question my own art-making, my writing processes. I had been writing in certain ways due to certain theories about deconstruction and decentralization. Especially in the novel I had just finished, *Don Quixote*. When I had first read Foucault and Deleuze and Guatteri and met Felix Guatteri, I knew that those philosophes were working as they were working for cultural and *political* reasons and purposes. At that time, Deleuze and Guatteri were deeply involved with the Autonomia in Italy. The Anglo-Saxon adoption and adaption of deconstruction had depoliticized the theories. It seems not by an act of chance that Jean Baudrillard, out of all those French theorists, became the theoretical idol of the New York art world, Baudrillard whose politics, unlike Deleuze's and Guatteri's, are, at best, dubious . . .

Suddenly and ironically, in this Anglo-Saxon climate, deconstructive, now known as postmodernist, techniques became methods for applauding the society and social values composed by American postindustrialization. Freed of Neitzchean *sovereignty*, any value or text could be equivalent to or substitute for any other value or text; meaning became a black hole and frivolity instead of humanism reigned . . .

In such a world, that of the collapse of all social value, the world of Watergate, where leaders of the polis commit major crimes and their behavior is deemed normal and acceptable, I wondered what art could be. What art is. I began to question, as I've said, all I had learned and composed.

Returning to New York City in January, hungry for New York's art community, or rather for my memory's vision of New York's art community, I ran from gallery to gallery. Sherri Levine, Richard Prince, Jenny Holzer, etc. Artists from whom I had learned much. I now saw that these works equaled money. Art was simply stock in a certain stock market; according to gallery dealers such as Richard Flood at Barbara Gladstone, the art stock market at its top levels was booming more than ever. Despite the general economic decline of the Wall Street market. The rich, as Richard put it, are still becoming richer.

I searched for younger or more radical work or just something other than stock. But the New York art world seemed to have closed its ranks: the old community in which an underground gradually became commercial has disintegrated into a market whose share-holders, frightened, are determined to take no more chances.

For New York City is a very expensive urban area. If one wants to stay alive. Not everyone does.

What I saw in New York in the past six months confirmed all my questionings about art. The nature of art in a degenerating polis inimical to all but its own centralized power. I have been asked tonight to speak about art criticism. Art criticism is writing about art. If, in a society that seems psychotic, art is questionable (I mean the word *questionable* in every possible sense): what can art criticism be?

Theoretical language in a patriarchal society

In order to examine a piece of art criticism, the relations between that critical work and the art works under surveyance, and perhaps most important, the relations between this criticism-work-of-art pair and the art and other contexts in which the art-art-criticism pair appears, to avoid any possible unfriendly reference to any art critic, I'm going to discuss a piece of criticism I recently penned.

In the spring of this year I was commissioned by the *Village Voice* to write a 3,000 to 4,000-word piece about Peter Greenaway's movies, especially about his most recent movie, *The Cook, the Thief, His Wife and Her Lover*.

My piece would be based on an interview with Greenaway. For

the *Voice* wasn't as interested in critical judgments on Greenaway's latest film as in as complete a presentation as possible of Greenaway's work, theories, and even private histories.

Until his most recent film, *The Cook, the Thief, His Wife and Her Lover*, Peter Greenaway's movies have been shown in the United States, if at all, only in American art movie houses. The first film, *The Draughtsman's Contract*, did fairly well here as an art movie. Especially considering that it was his first major film. *Zed and Two Noughts*, the next film, has hardly been shown; *Drowning by Numbers* has never been publicly presented in this country. Only one film, *The Belly of the Architect*, is available on VHS.

In England Greenaway is one of, probably the most famous, though not the most commercial, filmmaker of his generation.

Miramax, Greenaway's distributors in this country, and by the way, Almódovar's, prior to the writing of my article, believed that *The Cook, the Thief, His Wife and Her Lover* would be the breakthrough film for Greenaway in the United States. There had never been a major article on Greenaway's work in this country. Miramax, though very kind to me, made clear that my article could, in fact would, pave the way for the desired breakthrough.

Though in my article I had no interest in ranking, in judging Greenaway's films, the seriousness with which I discussed the themes in his work rested on the presupposition that Greenaway's opus is significant, well worth considering.

This, then, was the relation between my critical piece and Greenaway's art: I was the critical authority; as authority, I was stating the themes and deep meanings in his work and positioning these historically; my words verbally represented, stood for and in place of Greenaway's filmic images.

For Miramax, the purpose of this representation of Greenaway's art was to sell the new and then the earlier movies, to open up the Greenaway market. My purpose was to make the $1,200 that the *Voice* proposed to pay me for my piece. The *Voice*'s purposes were probably less specific and more complex: to sell papers and to support a cultural art, Greenaway's films. My *Voice* editor, Richard

Goldstein, who's a very fine man, has a high regard for Green-away's work.

Any artwork which is not propagandic and perhaps artwork which is, is ambiguous with regard to deep meaning. Art criticism must deny this ambiguity, so that the buyers know what to buy. So that the culture-mongers know what culture to eat. Those who deal in commerce do not want to, cannot afford to live in chaos.

Perhaps especially, moral chaos. We are now entering a period of economic collapse, economic chaos. This economic chaos by necessity is closely tied to political chaos. As an example, look at New York City. Our government, desperate to survive, to maintain its power, is trying to mask political and economic chaos by turning to and increasing political and moral repression, stricture, control. Morality, economics, and art are walking hand in hand.

Back to art. An artwork, any artwork, is ambiguous: its deep meanings are contradictory. The tensions resulting from these contradictions create a world and lead out into the world. Neither we, human, nor art live in a world of finite meaning finitude or are we or art finite in regard to meaning. Identity, fragile, gives way to identity. We and the world are finite only in regard to death. If that. As to art criticism: art criticism, as said, represents the pertinent work of art. The homogeneity of the criticism dis-simulates the heterogeneity of the art. Often for the purposes of the art market:

By means of the act of representing with authority, art criticism transforms a complex of meanings that do not have closure (the artwork) into a structure of closed or centralized meaning and defined position in culture and history. The relationship between artwork and art criticism, the society alluded to in this pairing, not represented but presented, is phallocentric, patriarchal. The society of judgment.

The homogeneity of the verbal criticism masks the heterogeneity of the art in the same way that in the "Nietzschean body politic, the homogeneity of the ego dissimulates the heterogeneity of the body; the ego, a function of language, organizes the . . . manifestations and expressions of the libido" (Weiss, *The Aesthetics of Excess*, p. 27).

The authoritative representing act isn't questionable simply because it lies. For fiction and fact are wedded. It is questionable because it is the transformation of all the multitudinous languages of the body into a judgmental language, the language of the logos. Critical language, language which denies ambiguity and exists primarily for other than itself, reifies the Descartian mind-body split by denying the existence of the body.

The language by means of which we represent ourselves as judges, as absolute knowers, is not the language of flux, of material, of that which must die. Us.

Over and over again, in our false acts of absolute judgment and criticism, we deny the realm of death. For its perverse head, Pluto, informs us that we cannot be authorities, that we will never know.

I want to talk about the body and the languages of the body. Which art criticism has denied. And about what art criticism could come out of the languages of the body.

To do this, I'll begin by describing a model of a person, a human, that is not Cartesian. From this model will arise, hopefully, possible models of art critical languages which, being of the body, no longer reduce difference to identity, radical difference to a schematic, controllable form.

Nonpatriarchal Language: The Body

"Acéphale" was the name of the "secret society" with which George Bataille worked from 1936 through 1939. M. Blanchot, the novelist, has said of Acéphale (the society): "Those who participated are not sure they ever took part in it." According to Denis de Rougemont: "*Acéphale* is the sign of radical antistatism, that is to say, of the only antifascism worthy of the name. This society, which has no single head, is more or less what, in less romantic terms, we call a federation. On this crucial point, it seems much easier to make Nietzsche and his disciples agree with personalism than with any other political doctrine."

This loose group produced a journal, also named *Acéphale*,

which, according to the philosopher and Klossowski's collaborator, Paul-Louis Landsberg, defended "the personal essence of a thought" that cannot be "separated from the life of a man or from the totality of his experience."

The acephalic god first appeared on a third- or fourth-century Gnostic stone, an abraxas. In Bataille's and Klossowski's version, this god, Acéphale, is headless. The elimination of the head, this forgetting, according to Bataille, "entails the exclusion of any quest for origins" (it is interesting that this was written during the Nazi days) and entails "the eradication of all identity."

Another form of Acéphale—there is no one *authoritative* image —is also headless; this time the head is a skull at the place of, in the place of, the genitalia. Here is the place where the logos ought to be or is. In personal language, the head is ruled by the cunt.

Moreover, the head is a skull. It is said that in the Middle Ages, monks contemplated skulls in order to see God or Truth. To see clearly is to perceive that one must die. The logos must realize that it is part of the body and that this body is limited. Subject, not to the mind, but to death. Here is the place of sex.

In this Acéphale's right hand, a heart sits in its own flames. This, not the head, is the topmost part of the body.

This Acéphale's left hand holds a sword. The sword is the emblem of violence and power which are necessary, not for slaughter, but for self-decapitation. The head must be cut off so that it, the Logos, the Platonic head, the ruler, can be set in his proper place.

Decapitation also must occur so that the fleshy passions, the flaming heart, freed of prison fetters, can burn into joy, jouissance. Holiday, which our society recognizes only in the form of a farce named Club Med.

"In the face of the weighty animality of death," Bataille wrote, "life appears avid with joy imperative."

The sword is also the will turned back on itself. Here Bataille is disputing Nietzche's "Will to Power." The sword, the will turns on, interiorizes or eats itself so that pure power turns into play. This play is the ground for art.

Art's realm, according to this picture or god, is not transcendence, but play in the world of change, the world of limitations, radical difference and Nietzchean "sovereignty."

Acephale's center is the colon; the colon is labyrinthine. In a labyrinth, reason is useless, lost. In the labyrinth, remember Borges's labyrinths, the self becomes lost. In the labyrinth, paths, ways of knowing, seem subject to chance. Chance or Fortune and chaos are simply those lands which lie outside and beyond our understanding.

When the colon or labyrinth is center, our center, we, human, learn how little, if anything, we know and can know. Since the law presupposes knowledge, we learn to distrust the law.

A colon's end is shit. Not transcendence, but waste. Beyond meaning. For the head is no longer the head; we live, perceive, and speak, in our bodies and through our bodies. There is no escape from that, us, which is subject to death and will become excrement—this is the Nietzchean "Eternal Return"—there is no escape from this labyrinth. The nature, the being of the body. We who pretend to know, to criticize, are frail, uncertain, and more ungainly than swans who have risen out of their natural element and are walking on solid ground.

This labyrinth is also the labyrinth of language. It is these languages that I want to begin to find.

I, Ariadne, enabled my lover to kill the monster in the center of the labyrinth and to escape that labyrinth. I, Ariadne, defeated the labyrinth made by the artist, Daedalus.

For the sake of love.

Then my lover abandoned me. Because he found someone else. Or because Dionysius, more powerful than my lover, wanted me, fucked me, then slew me.

I did not escape love's labyrinth.

This is the dream. The dream of the labyrinth or the self that will lead us to languages that cannot be authoritarian.

The Languages of the Body:

1. The languages of flux. Of uncertainty in which the 'I' (eye)

constantly changes. For the self is "an indefinite series of identities and transformations."

2. The languages of wonder, not of judgment. The eye (I) is continuously seeing new phenomena, for, like sailors, we travel through the world, through our selves, through worlds.

3. Languages which contradict themselves.

4. The languages of this material body: laughter, silence, screaming.

5. Scatology. That laughter.

6. The languages of play: poetry. Pier Paolo Pasolini decided to write in the Friulian dialect as "a mystic act of love . . . the central idea . . . was . . . (that) of the language of poetry as an absolute language."

7. Language that announces itself as insufficient.

8. Above all: the languages of intensity. Since the body's, our, end isn't transcendence but excrement, the life of the body exists as pure intensity. The sexual and emotive languages.

9. The only religions are scatology and intensity.

10. Language that forgets itself. For if we knew that chance governs us and this world, that would be absolute knowledge.

Then forget all of this. In the modes of silence: secrets, autism, forgettings, disavowals, even death. Let these be the languages of art criticism: to scream, to forget, to do anything except reduce radical difference, through representation, to identity, singularity, calculable and controllable.

Let one of art criticism's languages be silence so that we can hear the sounds of the body: the winds and voices from far-off shores, the sounds of the unknown.

May we write, not in order to judge, but for and in (I quote George Bataille), "the community of those who do not have a community."

1990

10. Moving Into Wonder

I am going to tell you a story. It is a shortened version of a much longer story, one in which there are no fictional elements. As they say, nothing here has been made up. It is also the story of the origin of art.

When humans understood that there were powers greater than themselves and so told myths rather than histories, the priestesses of Daphne or The Bloody One, for women enjoy their ability to menstruate, when this goddess was in an orgiastic mood, chewed laurel leaves and then, under a grown moon, assaulted unsuspecting travelers and tore children into pieces.

Daphne was also named Medusa. This face turned all men who looked on it into stone, this face made out of living cunt hair, and so kept strangers from trespassing into her mysteries.

Nevertheless some men loved her. One of them, Leucippus, the king of the horse cult, disguised himself as a woman so he could take part in her raptures. For this reason the god Apollo, for he also lusted after Daphne, hinted to her priestesses, the Maenads, that they should bathe naked. When they did so, they discovered one of them was a boy. They tore Leucippus's body into pieces.

Now Apollo felt that he was free to have Daphne. He found her and grabbed her, roughly. She called out to her mother. Earth took her Daphne away to Crete, for that was another home of the mysteries, and in her daughter's place, left a laurel-tree.

Apollo came up to this tree, saying, "Then you're mine." The laurel became the crown of the poet. For chewing on the laurel turns a human mad; poets often are insane.

In Crete, Daphne took another name. Pasiphae.

To ensure his holdings, Minos, the King of Crete, promised to sacrifice a bull to Poseidon, Lord of the Ocean. But when the Sea-God sent him a blindingly white bull for his offering, the king fell in love with the animal and kept him for himself.

Minos had already married Pasiphae.

Even though married, Pasiphae fell in love with this white bull; desperate to have sex with him, she ran for help to Daedalus, the artist. His art consisted of making animated wooden dolls. Feeling sympathy for Pasiphae, he built a hollow wooden cow for her, a moo-cow into which she could climb. She did, and Daedalus wheeled this animal into the section of oaks where all the other beasts were grazing.

Approaching the fake cow, the white bull raised himself up, then over the double-female and came in her.

Pasiphae gave birth to a child whose head was a bull's and whose body, human. Thus, a monster, for the head as the seat of reason is supposed to govern the body.

Minos visited an oracle. "How can I keep everyone from knowing about my wife's lust? How can I hide this monstrosity?"

Oracular answer: "Tell Daedalus, that artist who's living under your protectorate, to construct a labyrinth! A labyrinth is that structure from which no one can escape. In its center, place Pasiphae and her child or monster, the Minotaur."

Minos did as he was told by the oracle of Apollo, the chewer of laurel leaves.

Now the labyrinth has been constructed.

It will be Ariadne, the daughter who, like her mother, lusts, in

Ariadne's case, unnaturally lusts for a human, Ariadne who opens up the labyrinth. By following lust or love. Unfortunately for all who are Cretan including Ariadne, she opens up the labyrinth to a stranger, a man whose only desire is to murder.

The stranger, Theseus, slays the monster. Monster comes from the Latin word *monstrum* or wonder. It is Ariadne, then, whose lust allows the destruction of wonder:

"When Theseus emerged from the labyrinth, spotted with the Minotaur's blood, Ariadne embraced him passionately." Theseus proceeds to desert Ariadne.

Already the mother had disappeared from the story.

The mother speaks:

The labyrinth:

This is a series of rooms without end or beginning. Not a circle, no, but a hexagon, a form like that. Afterward all I remembered was white dust.

The center of the labyrinth:

The large room or the front room. It's all light here; all the light comes from here: floors made out of dust and grays and pale browns. This is the kind of day in which nothing grows. The center of the labyrinth is a hairdresser's. Someone—he must be the monster—asks me to get something for him while he's gone so I leave this room of light and start to walk down a hall the angles of whose junctures are those of a hexagonal.

Now the dust is white because everything, walls and floor, are becoming drier. When dust dries, it disintegrates into nothing. There are more dust and insects in the walls. In the final room to which I'm capable of walking, spiders are living in a mattress. There might be more spiders than mattress here.

I run away, back the way I came. In the middle of the hall sections which now lie in a straight line, there's a place where I can go swimming. A pool found in an old, old hotel. The amount of insects has grown so great that even when I'm back where I started, in the room of light, all I want to do is escape.

How I escape from the labyrinth:

In a bathroom, I'm popping a pimple which, as I look at it in a mirror after the first popping try, grows larger and larger so I see that it is rising up. I see a small cylinder shape that's almost solid. Like a missile. Then I remember that when I did this before, I didn't damage my skin permanently. As the little cock rises and rises, I feel good.

This time when I return, perhaps because of the pimple, the sea lies in front of my eyes.

A world of wonder:

Colors more brilliant than the usual colors of the world begin to be:

Two ships are lying on green, deep waters. These vessels are like the ones pirates used to have. A ship/man, his head is a ship and his body, a man's, is walking over the sands in front of the water. I know that he's meant for me because both the colors and the shapes of this being and of the ships are more precise than any color or shape before this and because they are going to take me, finally, away from the land.

On a ship in the middle of the ocean. I see there are fish swimming all around its wood sides. When I look more carefully, I see that all the fish are one fish. A baby 'cause it's fatter than every other fish. It leaps out of the water so that I can pet it. I'm able to lift it out of the water 'cause a man, a fisherman, is helping me. Then, I put the creature back in the water and before I can know anything, an even larger sea-animal comes swimming over. It's the baby's mommy and I'm so glad she's now happy and her child swims into her mouth and she swims away.

I see even larger fish, daddy fish, like whales. Seeing them enables me to feed them. I shovel huge balls of hamburger and grapefruit into one of the daddy fish's mouth. All stories are true. I tell you this. No story, unless it is made up by one person, can be false. For as soon as something is told to another person, it begins to exist.

At every motion or moment of time, all that exists begins and simultaneously ends. For time is not linear.

According to this story, the first human artist was Daedalus. Was a male. Was, as artist, both inferior and subject to the representative of political power. Daedalus lived in exile; his survival depended upon the goodwill of King Minos. The realm of art was separate from and subservient to that of the political.

If Daedalus was the first artist, art began out of division. The word art began to be used as soon as there was separation between imagination and state.

Prior to Apollo's rape of Daphne and to Apollo's reign, there was no such division. When Daphne and the Maenads danced, imagination became actual.

The labyrinth, that construction of Daedalus's, covered up the origin of art. Covered up the knowledge that art was, and so is, born out of rape or the denial of women and born out of political hegemony.

One form of Daedalus's construction is time. When time is understood as linear, there is no escape. No escape for us out of the labyrinth. I said that the labyrinth has been built.

But time is not only linear. Unlike Ariadne, for we do not hold Theseus as our lover, let us, by changing the linearity of time, deconstruct the labyrinth and see what the women who are in its center are doing. Let us see what is now central.

1995

11. Writing, Identity, and Copyright in the Net Age

In my confusion, I look to older writing, as I have often done when I am confused. I look to find a clue about my own writing.

Unfortunately, the school systems in this country are being allotted less and less government funding. I will regret if the culture of our society, through the loss of education, loses its sense of history. I shall regret if those who are involved in culture no longer think historically, if they no longer turn to their, to our histories for models, for examples.

Looking, I turned to the writings of Hannah Arendt, a philosopher whose thinking is deeply embedded in the historical. "Even those among us," Arendt writes, "who by speaking and writing have ventured into public life have not done so out of any original pleasure in the public scene, and have hardly expected or aspired to receive the stamp of public approval." And she continues, and now she is truly beginning to help me, ". . . even in public they [those among us] tended to address only their friends and to speak to those unknown, scattered readers and listeners with whom everyone who speaks and writes at all cannot help feeling joined in some rather obscure brotherhood." As I continue to read, her words clarify more and more of what I, and perhaps many of you, are feeling right now. And perhaps this is how literature works: "I am afraid that in their efforts, they felt very little responsibility toward the world; these efforts were, rather, guided by their hope of preserving some minimum of humanity in a world grown inhuman while at the same time as far as possible resisting the weird irreality of this worldlessness—each after his own fashion and some few by seeking to the limits of their ability to understand even inhumanity and the intellectual and political monstrosities of a time out of joint."

The Task of a Writer

This is what I want to talk about: a time out of joint. The name of the collection of essays from which I've borrowed, which I've used, these bits of Arendt's writing are from *Men in Dark Times*.

For many of us, these are dark times. Are they harder or easier than the times in which and about which Hannah Arendt wrote? A useless question.

Certainly these times are hard, if not for us, then for our friends. If not for our friends, then look at the streets, the homeless, the ghettoes, incurable diseases, the persistent if not increasing presence of racism, homophobia, of prejudice heaped upon prejudice and hatred upon hatred, worse, fear upon fear. We are aware that we know both and, perhaps, are both victim and victimizer. For historically we have and still do participate in so many of the ownerships in this world.

We can throw away history, our history, as we seem to be trying to throw away education for all but the rich. But if we do throw history away, if we do not accept historical thinking, what kind of civilization are we negotiating? What kind of culture? If we throw history away, we are depriving ourselves of potentialities, potentialities for actions. Models and paradigms for actions. Potentiality is kin, and I am talking politically, kin to the imagination.

If we don't throw history away, if we think historically, what do we do about the hardships, the sufferings that we both experience and cause? Hannah Arendt suggests that the meaning of a "committed act," that is her phrase, is revealed only when the action itself has come to an end and become a story susceptible to narration. That is, "insofar as any *mastery* of the past is possible," thus, insofar as any mastery of suffering is possible, "it consists in relating what has happened."

When Arendt talks about story, about narration and narrative, she is not talking about a *master narrative*. She is talking about language as it moves from one point to another point. She is talking about meaning as it reveals itself and so is co-equivalent to language.

Arendt knows that writing, narration, does not end suffering: writing masters nothing. Narration, writing does something else. It restores meaning to a world which hardship and suffering have revealed as chaotic and senseless.

Hard Times

But what if times are really hard? So hard that the very existence of writing, which bestows humanity, is in danger? The loss, not of art, but of community, the loss of history and of writing as the ground of history— that loss in this world is a kind of death.

If we look at the literary industry today, writing is in trouble. Very few writers who spend most of their time writing and those who want to spend most of their time writing, can make a living by doing what they do most of the time and by what they love to do most. Those who can and do support themselves writing do so, on the whole, by virtue of something called *copyright*. Copyright's existence, I believe, is based on the following assumptions or sentences: *An author is the only person who has written her or his own work; an author owns her or his own work.*

Now in the first sentence—*an author is the only person who has written his or her own work*—the assumed definition of identity is questionable. For instance, I do not write out of nothing, or from nothing, for I must write with the help of other texts, be these texts written ones, oral ones, those of memory, those of dream, etc. In the second sentence, *an author owns her or his own work*, the verb to *own* must be questioned.

In other words, as writers we depend economically on copyright, its existence, because we are living and working, whether we like it or not, in a bourgeois-industrialist, in a capitalist society, a society based on ownership. One needs to own in order to survive, in fact, in order to be.

Our society, however, is in the process of, or has already changed into, a postindustrial ex-national economic beast. I hope that I am saying this correctly. As economic grounds change, so do all others. Both language and communications and the place of language and of communications in our society are rapidly changing.

For instance: I teach writing courses at the San Francisco Art Institute. Each year, fewer and fewer of my students read books. I don't mean that they don't read. They do, though they might not admit it. They read magazines, 'zines, they go to art performances, to spoken word events; they eagerly participate in such events; they buy CDs in which rock starts and poets perform. More and more students and, I might add, my friends, and myself are using the Internet as a location where we can place our work. For the moment, the Net is a free zone . . . for those who can afford or access the necessary equipment. Whether it will remain free or whether our government will be able to enact strict controls, or whether various multinational corporations will be able to turn the Net into a cross between TV media land and a shopping mall, an elephantine version of America Online, this no one knows. Certainly, there are those who think that the Net cannot be controlled. Now, I have no ideas whether or not it will be, that is, whether or not it can be. But either way, there is one thing I suspect. I suspect that *copyright* as we now define it will become a thing of the past.

I have taken a long-winded route to make one simple point, something that I think most writers now know: if it is at this historical moment difficult for a writer to make a living by depending on *copyright*, in the future it may prove impossible for all but the very, very few.

It is not the case that the Net is providing an alternative method of book publishing and distribution. Not at the moment, as the technology stands. No one is going to download a whole book, for it's far easier to run to the nearest bookstore. The existence of the Net is threatening the literary industry in another way: my students, people who work, which probably means that they work more than eight hours a day and have little time to read, many, many of the people in this society are preferring to engage in writing and in writerly activities outside the realm of books. And so to a large extent, outside the realm of *copyright*, as *copyright* now exists. These are indeed hard times.

Without Copyright

If we get rid of *copyright* as it now exists, do we have to throw writing away?

In order to answer this question, I think that it's necessary to try to see clearly, to see the society in which we're living. I should say *societies*, for sometimes the only entities that make our societies single seem to be McDonald's hamburgers and Madonna. We need to see how we as writers fit into our societies as and while these societies are changing. How can we, as Hannah Arendt says, even in worlds that seem to have become inhuman, remain obligated to these worlds? *Obligated*, for being writers, our job is to hear and put together narrations and so to give meaning even to what seems to be or is inhuman.

How can I, as a writer, be of use to and in my societies? That is the question that underlies the one of *copyright*.

I think that it is hard to understand what writing is in our society because writing has become so entangled with the literary industry. Entangled to the point that there no longer seems to be any difference between the two. For instance, if a writer is not *big business*, she or he is not a good, that is, finally, not a *publishable* writer.

Let me paraphrase and so repeat Hannah Arendt's question: To what extent do we remain obligated to a world even when our presence is no longer desired in that world? Are we, writers, obligated to the literary industry and to the society behind that industry? Here is Hannah Arendt's answer: "Flight from the world in dark times of impotence can always be justified as long as reality is not ignored." *Flight* does not mean *abandonment*.

As it now stands, the literary industry depends upon *copyright*. But not literature. Euripides, for instance, wrote his version of Electra while Sophocles's "copyright" was still active. *Not* to mention Shakespeare's, Marlowe's, and Ford's use of each other's texts. My worries with *copyright*, however, are not so academic. My worries concern the increasing marginalization of writers and of their writings in this society. Whenever writers are considered marginal to a society, something is deeply wrong, wrong in that society and wrong with the relations between writing and the society. For *to write* should be *to write the world* and, simultaneously, *to engage in the world*. But the literary industry as it now exists seems to be obfuscating relations between this society's writers and this society.

Once more we need to see what writing is. We need to step away from all the business. We need to step to the personal. This is what I mean by *flight*. Business has become too heavy, too dominant. We need to remember friends, that we write deeply out of friendship, that we write to friends. We need to regain some of the energy, as writers and as readers, that people have on the Internet when for the first time they e-mail, when they discover that they can write anything, even to a stranger, even the most personal of matters. When they discover that strangers can communicate to each other.

The bestowing of meaning and, thus, the making of the world, the word as world: this is what writing is about.

Friendship

In our society, the excitement, the energy, and the power is no longer located in writing, that is, in the writing world. The excitement is found in film, as in *Pulp Fiction*, or in the TV of David Lynch. Perhaps we should ask why the writing industry, in terms of the overall culture, is emasculated. (I should say, *e-femin-ated*.)

Back to Hannah Arendt's words. You see, my lazy mind never

goes anywhere: it only returns. Writing, as defined by the literary industry, is all about individuals. *I own my writing; that is copyright.* "Power arises," Arendt writes, "only where people act together, not where people grow stronger as individuals."

To write is to do other than announce oneself as an enclosed individual. Even the most narcissist of texts, say Nabokov's *Lolita*, reaches out to, in *Lolita*'s case grabs at, its reader. To write is to write to another. Not *for another*, as if one could take away that other's otherness, but *to another*. To write, as Gertrude Stein and Maurice Blanchot both have said, is to write to a stranger, to a friend. As we go forward, say on the Net, perhaps we are also going back, and I am not a great believer in linear models of time, to times when literature and economics met each other in the region of friendship. "The ancients," comments Arendt, "thought friends indispensable to human life, indeed that a life without friends was not really worth living."

Friendship is always a political act, for it unites citizens into a *polis*, a (political) community. And it is this friendship that the existence of copyright (as it is now defined) has obfuscated.

The loss of friendship, the giving over of friendship to business based on individualism, has caused loss of energy in the literary world. Think, for a moment, with how much more energy one does something for a lover or for a close friend than when one acts only in the service of oneself.

In his remarkable essay about the writings of his friend Georges Bataille, Maurice Blanchot opposes two kinds of relationships, that of friendship and that of totalitarianism. Both Blanchot and Bataille lived through Nazism and Stalinism. A totalitarian relationship, Blanchot states, is one in which the subject denies the otherness, therefore the very existence of the other person, the person to whom he or she is talking. Thus, the totalitarian relationship is built upon individualism as closure. Individualism as the closing down of energy, of meaning. Whereas, when I talk to my friend, when I write to her, I am writing to someone whose otherness I accept. It is the difference between me and my friend that allows meaning; meaning begins in this difference. And it is meaning, the meaningfulness of the world, that is consciousness. You see, I am finally talking about my writing.

1995

12. | The City

Russian Constructivism

1. Abstraction

Petersburg, my city.

Petersburg steeples triangles bums on the streets decrepit churches broken-down churches churches gone churches used as homes for bums for children forced from the abandoned buildings they run.

Son.

1.

City of people who weren't born here who decided to live here who're homeless, trying to make their own lives: poor refugees artists rich people. People who don't care and care too much. Homeless. You, baby crib, only you've been financially shuffled off by the USSR government.

You, city, along one of whose streets a hundred bums're sitting standing and lying. Three-quarters of these bums're black or Puerto Rican. The concrete stinks of piss much more than the surrounding streets smell. A few of the creeps smoke cigarettes. One-half of the buildings lining the street're a red brick wall. Mostly the bums don't move or they move as little as they have to.

How is this City of Cities divided?

This new holy city is a reality not only without religion but also without anything to want or seek for: without anything. The city whose first characteristic is it gives nothing, breakdown, and so its inhabitants individuals, no its communities, have to make everything for themselves.

As taught in school, Petersburg has five parts: its main part is the Nevsky Prospect.

St. Petersburg is actually the Nevsky Prospect.

The Nevsky Prospect's an island joined by bridges once on its northern tip, twice on its southern, and once at its eastern edge to the rest of Petersburg. Though Petersburg is the capital of the USSR, most Russians who don't live in Petersburg hate and fear the Petersburgians: they think they're murderers, dope addicts, and perverted by fame.

Lamplights hang over the edges of the park running through the vertical center of the Nevsky Prospect, from its beginning at St. Isaac's, about fifty blocks north, to its black section in the depth of the seventeenth line. The geographical divisions are actually racial: ghettoes, each one on the whole about nine to sixteen blocks large, don't mingle. This past year the ghettoes're beginning to physically cross 'cause the rich're now trying and will take over this whole city by buying all of its real estate.

The islands especially Vasilyevsky Island are the drug oases. The hooker's centers're the Millionaya, again Vasilyevsky Island (pimps always get their puppets hooked), the large black bridge across the Neva, and the Winter Canal. The languages are less than 50 percent Russian, then (heard less often in this order) Spanish, French, and German. Petersburg isn't Russian: it's a country on its own. Since it has no legal or financial national status, it's an impossibility, an impossible home; it's tenuous, paranoid. Its definitions and language're quantum theory, Zen, and the nihilism found before the Russian Revolution.

Squares quadrilaterals concatenations of imaginations who lack other necessary sensualities. The flesh which touches flesh has to resemble Martian green gook. City of simultaneous inner and outer space where each day a new human disease appears, whose inhabitants, like rats, through sickness remain alive and work. Who can tell me I'm too sick to be alive? My sickness is life. You, my city, romanticism of no possible belief:

In Peter one morning, the female weightlifter fell out of her loft-bed. It was a beautiful day, late in September. Larks were singing and drops of sunlight were filtering through the navy blue Levelors (through the clouds through the pollution through the surrounding buildings' walls) which she hadn't opened since she bought them 'cause she didn't want to see junkies shooting up.

A newspaper below her fallen body:

CITY OF PASSION

a non-achiever	George was totally wrapp
non-leader, non-	up in the fantasy world
and non-romantic,'	comic books.
former classmate	'He was also cons
lentine.	with TV—especiall
he was 18, George	ture shows,' said
stined to end up a	By high scho
then a horrifying	had withdrawn

Meanwhile, in the alleyways,

Dear Peter,

I can't stand living without you. I hate this day-after-day constant waiting-for-you: you're not here: all my hours spent in longing for what's not here. I won't stand for living like this. Then I realize I'm falling in love with you. There's no one to turn to: again and again I realize I have only myself.

Sixteen hours until I see you again. 1 2 3 4 5 6 7 8 9 10 11 12 13 14 15 16. I can count 16, but you'll probably not want to see me. If I see you, I'll want you. If I don't see you, I'll die. I'm going nuts. I don't care about this writing. I just want time. I can get rid of this night by closing up my eyes with work, brain calculations,

dumbie-making TV: you have leapt into my arms, madness: I'll
wait for you forever if you'll only come to me, for there's no time
until I see you. Love makes time and life. I must be blind: you're
poor. Your life is shambles. The more you want something, the
more you deny it to yourself. You: my nightmare; I don't care.
You've conquered me. You, kookoo totally untogether, make me
as irritable and changeable as you are, so I've made myself into
your Rock of Gibraltar in order to capture you but I don't want
you, I don't want you to break up your marriage, I don't want you
to do anything that'll hurt you: I have to lose. But if you don't see
me tomorrow, I don't have to lose because you don't love me. So:
real love is strange and any simplicity between us has to be a lie.

I don't know what I'm doing. You're the only life I've known in
a very long time. How can I let go of life again? You're my day
and night. Forget it, little baby, he's told you clearly he doesn't
want to have sex with you and he only wants you so he can revenge
himself on his wife 'cause she once left him for a richer man. You
are my madness. Come in me, my madness, and since you've
already taken me, I beg you with everything that is me to take me.
I'm sold, but not yet enjoyed. The day I'm going to see you I'm
happy and the day I'm not going to see you I'm miserable. (My
nurse enters and binds me up.)

Nurse: Shut up, brat.

Myself, to Myself: I don't talk 'cause I can't talk about you. I
guess I am obsessed possessed. Spain needed a revolution, a far
more profound revolution in fact than that being attempted by the
Republic. I'm bound by cords 'cause you aren't fucking me. (Aloud,
((Allowed))) Cords're binding me 'cause you aren't fucking me.
You're going away from me.

Juliet: You're going away from me. It's still dark and black and
hideous: you don't have to leave me yet.

You: It is daytime; there are candles. The beginnings of clouds
can be seen. Since this world for her light no longer needs the
stars, like the jealous bitch she is, she's shut them off. Day like
total revolution's waiting to infiltrate. I have to get away from you
to keep my life going.

Juliet: The light that's coming within you for me's as violent as mine for you. As you say we've nothing to do with nature: the fire between us competes with the sun. I'll keep your unnatural solitary fire going! I'll follow you in disguise. You don't need to ever leave me. Don't go.

You: Okay. I'll stay with you and I'll die. I give way to your love: These beginning light lines in the sky are the streaks of blood on your colorless unspeakable thighs. The unseeable approaching daylight isn't a day but just moon to your energy and grace. Since without you I die and with you I die, I chose to die with you, my life, and besides, I've no choice. It's dark and black and hideous still.

Juliet, resigning herself: Go. Get out. This world stinks. We can't pretend this world doesn't exist. The Fascists have taken over. All that's natural and beautiful're dividing us. Since natural is now unnatural and unnatural is natural, those who love can't know. How should I know what to do? It is the day: get away from me!

Dear Peter,

Please understand me. Please believe what's in my mind at this very moment. I do everything you want. Now you want to be away from me 'cause you're fucking your wife. You're the only one I love and this moment's infinite. I'd do anything to phone you right now. 'Cause I can't phone you, I hate you. 'Cause I hate you, I'm never going to phone you ever again, 'cause I hate you. I'll say your name so the whole world'll know, 'cause what you fear most, your only morality, is what you think other people (whether or not they know you)'re thinking of you. King Sunny Adé. King Sunny Adé, I hate your guts. You were my sun and your house was my house was my home and you threw me out like a kid without a home (you), saying, "All you want is security so you don't love me at all," and then you didn't even understand that I love you. That's why this moment's infinite.

Why do I like you 'cause I know you're so self-righteous you'd holocaust the universe faster than Margaret Thatcher; you don't understand what art is 'cause you're so scared of your wildness with which, you artist, you're frothing, you're trying to eradicate every weakness mainly those in other people 'cause that's what you see so you demand certain behaviors and accept nothing else; when people act differently, 'cause you've buried your wildnesses more anger volcanoes out of you than I've ever felt from another human being? I like you 'cause your eyes look at me a certain way and 'cause your nose twitches; your mental capacities're at least as sharp and rapid as mine; when you're not being (ridiculously) ruled, you're as decadent as I am. Why do you give a damn about social rules? Why not become an artist? I'm going to fuck lots of men now if they'll fuck me 'cause I need that physical reassurance and I'm sure while I'm doing this, there'll still be thoughts of our fucking.

Between you and me was a madness which's rare. Not just sexuality. Who're you kidding? That this anger and fear (appearing 'cause I touched your madness too closely or 'cause you care about society) are more powerful than your sexuality? Only a man who adores fucking comes near me. What's love? Love's the unity of friendship and desire. I messed up with you. I didn't care enough about friendship. I fought too hard against your desire to be socialized which, if I love you, should be as important to me as my ways. Can you be patient?—I'm willing to fight myself to be with you.

You don't think our friendship's important. Maybe you're so young, you believe there're an infinite number of mad relations.

I agree with you: I was too frightened you didn't love me and not terrified enough of imposing on your love. Please remember, you also feared I didn't love you and you begged me for reassurance.

I hope your wife'll make you happy forever. I'm saying this 'cause I want to be friends. I want my desire for friendship to waken your love for me—

Walking the streets.

Tatlin designed a city. Tatlin took unhandlable passion and molded it.

It all comes out of passion. Our city of passion.

Biely wanted to fuck his closest comrade, Alexander Blok's wife until the duel between them in 1906 (which never happened), then Biely left Russia for a year. When Biely described this passion, he constructed language as if it was a building. If architecture wasn't cool cold, people couldn't live in it. I have to figure out why I'm hurting so much. Recognition: I'm really hurting. One of this hurt's preconditions is I'm in love with you.

A city in which we can live.

What're the materials of this city?

Is sensuality less valuable than rational thought? Is there a split between mind and body, or rather between these two types of mentality? Why's a cubist painting, if it is, better art than a Vivienne Westwood dress? Is our city abstract?

When you talk to me on the phone I'm hurt and maddened by your lack of sexual and emotional communication. Art criticism, unlike art,'s abstract.

I'll mold my love for you: I can't say over the telephone what I want to say to you: "Please touch your cock because I can't touch your cock now and I have to touch your cock." What's mainly not allowed? Time's the main non-allower. I can't touch your cock right now because one event can't be another event. (Time is substance.) Three thousand miles now between the events of you and me, or three hours. Absence to a child is death. This is death. Time's killing me. Time's proving you don't love me. I have to mold my passion for you out of time:

2. The Poems of a City
ON TIME

desinas ineptire et quod vides perisse perditum ducas.

fulsere quondam candidi tibi soles,
cum it hurts me to remember I did
act up today, a way of saying
"I'm not perfect," forgive my
phone call, ventiabas quo puella

The subjective mood takes precedence over the straight-forward active. The past controls the present. The past.

*ducebat (on a leash: leather
  Rome)*
*amata nobis quantum amabitur
nulla.*

The first future tense. What do
words really say: does this future propose future time?

*ibi illa multa kisses on kisses
  between us
your hands your flesh unending
  time into time
the past wasn't past—how do I
  transform the past: that awful
  prison 'cause it ends?
fulsere vere candidi tibi soles.*

By repeating the past, I'm mold-
ing and transforming it, an impossible act.

New section:

*nunc iam illa non vult: tu quoque,
  impotens can't fuck any boyfriends
  these days, bad mood no wonder
I'm acting badly, noli NO
nec quae fugit sectare, nec miser
  vive
good advice sed obstinata mente
  perfer, obdura.
vale, puella. (My awful telephone
  call. This's my apology, Peter.
  Do you accept?) iam (ha ha)
  Catullus obdurat,
nec te requiret nec rogabit invitam:
    I'm a good girl
I have, behave perfectly.
at tu dolebis. The imaginary makes
  reality, as in love, cum rogaberis
  nulla
scelesta. Scelesta nocte. My night.*

My present is negative. This
present becomes imaginary: The
future of amabitur and the subjunctive at the beginning of the
poem?:

quae tibi manet vita without me?
quis nunc adibit? without me cui
  videberis bella?
quem nunc amabis? with me you
  fuck whoever you want.
Let the imagination reign supreme.
  quem you now fucking? cuius esse
  diceris huh!
quem basiabis a stupid question? cui
  labella labula mordebis? (allied to
  death?)
at tu, Catullus, destinatus obdura
to facts, for only the imagination
  lives.

The imagination is will.

WILL VERSUS CHANCE
   no more sighing blackness nihilism
and senile old fogies' blathers
as snot falls out of their nostrils
all more worthless than the two bums I saw talking today.
suns rise and set I never see them—
for you my love and me a few brief hours of sun
then no consciousness blackness perpetually.
take it kiss me do it grab me
grab my arms grab my ankles grab my cunt hairs
the only nights of light the only eyes we have.
conscious.
so much so much so many phenomena we can no longer think
understand, realizing we're not responsible,
so no bourgeois or moralist can touch us
or know anything real about us.

TIME IS IDENTITY
   No one he states my boyfriend'ld rather fuck

than a duck, than me. Even if Psyche her—
self begged him. He said to me. But what a man tells any
woman who loves him is lost in these winds and squalling
waters. My lover is changing water.

LONELINESS

Lines one through four. Emotional thesis: on always being away
from you. I'm not scared of dying. I fear dying (absolute absence)'ll
take away your love for me.

Lines five and six. The supplementary thesis: death or absence
destroys love.

Lines seven through ten. The antithesis: love can and does fight
this absence.

Lines eleven and twelve. The synthesis: my love for you is
making me your mirror your object, fuses, whether I'm with or
away from you. So this love's overcoming and becoming, through
identity, one with death.

Lines thirteen through eighteen. The next thesis is based on the
above synthesis: when I'm dead and absolutely apart from you, I'll
still love you. No matter how long you stay alive, we'll eventually
be together forever.

Lines nineteen and twenty. The supplementary thesis: our love
is absence.

Lines twenty-one through twenty-four (the first section which
isn't just one whole sentence; the three short sentences of this
section syntactically reflect their verbal content). The antithesis:
this life or these constant changes may destroy our love. Like death,
love is infinite.

Lines twenty-five and twenty-six. The synthesis: while we're
alive right now we have to love each other as much as possible
'cause love has nothing to do with time. (I can never say anything
this direct to you 'cause I love you too much.)

The overall sentence syntactical structure is and concerns the
relations between several kinds of time. What is the verb structure?
Verbs're Latin's grammatical backbone.

The first kind of time, lines one through four, is linear time. The first main verb is *is*, an *is* which isn't Platonic. This common *is* leads to the first person subjunctives, *fear* and *hinder*, as well as the *is* subject noun, *fear*. This kind of time or the world makes human fear.

Common time's other or enemy is death. *Is* is bounded by death. So the other of *is* is *be without* in the present tense.

Since the past is like the present in this time model, lines five and six, death or absence also destroys memory. Here's another reason I'm afraid.

Since the only certainty I can have in common human time is that which has to be most feared—the end of time—all I can feel is more and more pain.

The second temporal model begins with human will, when I will to enter the realm of death. Line seven. This is exactly what I can't do, the antithesis, the necessarily imaginary.

Because we're apart, our sex because it has to continue, is false, imaginary. Line nine. Love makes me dare. I'm coming, masturbating, in the darkness. Line ten. Blind. Because I love you I want to die. My main verb is *orgasm* in the mythological past tense; in the realm of blackness the mythological's more powerful than the temporal present. (What is the time model of my will?)

If I've died to you, if I am dead, who am I? Because I love you I've destroyed myself: I'm you. Lines eleven and twelve. Love destroys common time and reverses subject and object; the verb acts on itself; I'm your mirror; identity's gone because there's no separation between life and death. Line twelve. The final model of time is that the mirror reflects the mirror: time is our love.

But my whole body's aching and I'm crying uncontrollably every night because you're not here:

Now all tenses and moods, *may come had given*, like and equal to all other phenomena appear out of nothing or death, line eighteen, which is also the ideal, lines fifteen and sixteen. But my whole body's aching and I'm crying uncontrollably every night because you're not here.

Now all tenses and moods, may come had given, like and equal to all other phenomena appear out of nothing or death, line eighteen, which is also the ideal, lines fifteen and sixteen. But my whole body's aching and I'm crying uncontrollably every night because you're not here, lines nineteen and twenty. The subjunctive tenses grammatically reflect this new model of common time: change is time.

I'm fighting the phenomenal that has to happen. I'm scared. Line twenty-one. So all the verbs are now subjunctives; all verbs are change. Again: loving you is making me feel pain. The final verb, *is changed*, grammatically reflects its opposite in content: the mirror. Time: love or fusion exists side by side with change:

I want you. That's all I can think. This is our absolute present. Line twenty-six.

TIME IS PAIN

last night I couldn't sleep at all, then I woke up in a sweat
though I wasn't crying tears fall from my eyes. I'm
in pain I phone you I want to suicide you
over and over again my brain revolves you
focus obsession I see nothing else. You're my world
blindness' opening my heart. This "love"
between us (your name) to me is *blood*.
Everywhere you slept you touched you came
in this house is your blood.
I would do anything to fall asleep. At night. But as
each dream passes
each absolute reality shows itself temporary
I obsess you. At times I hurt
like hell. At times I'm dead. Every other night
there's been a morning when I can
stand up from this bed.
Now there's only night: each night
unnatural is the ornament of your blood.

TIME IS MADE BY HUMANS

I hope there's some relief writing
this you: otherwise, none. I've never felt such pain.
Day after day pain after pain how do
I count these days? It's pain to count.
Pain to have a mind.
Worst: at the moment when sleep's ease should come,
(no coming. no you.) and thoughts are loosened,
but I don't want these thoughts.
I phone: I don't like life.
So stopping the mind up, no
life no utterance, jail within jail within
jail, what can days dates
time matter? Only this ease
of verbally sobbing out ugliness.

3. Scenes of Hope and Despair

The girl's happy because she knows the man she loves's in love with her.

The girl's sitting around: Peter didn't call me. You've got a date tomorrow with him, don't you? Should we eat? Did they fuck yet? Great fun, seducing girls. These men have the most fun. The most we can have is getting revenge. That is fun. Did they fuck yet? I don't know. Peter still hasn't called. I bet he forgets his accent. Uh-oh. Hurry back. Oh oh, she's drinking champagne. That means she's in love. I say, men just want you to suffer. They're so fucked up. They not only break up with you suddenly, they want this big dramatic thing. After you've broken up whenever a man starts talking about who's guilty, I tell him I couldn't care less I'd rather drink champagne. I think Peter's a little lame I mean he's always making dates and kind of forgetting the time but at the same time I could tell he really cared for me so his not calling me now doesn't mean he's off me. Edward's breaking up with me has made me think a man can't want me. All she does is cry. Englishmen fall in love too often so it doesn't mean anything to them. We always tell Englishmen, we only go with American men. This film is dumb.

Why do you want? I want love. You're not going to get love. Okay. You're going to get hurt again. I know. The main thing is to always giggle. All the last week when I really hurt, I felt like I had a disease. Being hurt is having a disease.

The girls cross their legs and laugh. "What should we do now?" "I need food," she, fainting, said. Her arms draped over the pillow. "We're caught in our own trap," she said laughing.

Right now the first girl is thinking about the man she wants to fuck. "We can," she says to her friend, "by fantasizing, increase our possibilities and joy in living, more important, understand how things work. Why's this? Examine these two events: 1. Last night I fucked with you. 2. I'm fantasizing fucking with you. But these events are now only my mentalities. Therefore there's no distinguishing between the two of them. But what if we hadn't fucked? Take another example: We don't love each other. Is it possible that by fantasizing we love each other, we can love each other? Possibly? Fantasy is or makes possibilities. Are possibilities reality?

The other girl lay in her red bed and crossed her legs. "There's always possibilities," she said. "I always prefer drama."

"I fantasize I desire and know what desire is. This's how fantasizing allows me to understand. Every possibility doesn't become actual fact. So knowing is separate from acting in the common world."

"I'm caught in my own trap 'cause every event for me can only be my mentality." The girls looked at each other.

"I know you know a good many of my New York friends and I've always wanted to talk with you about your work." "Come inside." "Are you reading Husserl?" "After college I was a political theorist. Then I worked for Austin." "Ooo. What's he like?"

What did we talk about?

"What's the relation between practice and theory in your film-making? I mean: does writing criticism stop you from making films?" "They're just two different kinds of activities." "But they're also two different ways of thinking." "When I made a film, probably partially because I always work with other people and also due to the film's economic situation, I know even before I start to make the film exactly what I'm going to do in the film." "Ugh: If I knew what I was going to write before I wrote a book, I'd be bored." "It's a different business. When you make a film, you have to consider who's going to see the film the popular culture." "Why do you care so much when you work how other people'll judge your work? I first consider my own pleasure? Do you think there's something fishy in the semiotics theories, especially in Deleuze's and Guattari's?" "There's a gap now. You have to realize that semiotics hit England before it hit America. We got Lacan and Althusser, rather than the later semioticians ... Derrida ... Foucault ..." "Foucault isn't really a semiotician. He was always on the outside. Who, then, 're you reading now?" "I have a theory that we're at the end of a generation. Semiotics's no longer applicable. At the moment there's nothing." "I remember in New York when semiotics came only it was Sylvere who brought it over, what it really did was give me a language with which I could speak about my work. Before that I had no way of discussing what I did, of course I did it, and my friends who are doing similar work we had no way of talking to each other. A critical way of talking about my work allowed me to go one step further in my work. Now it seems, as in the pre-semiotics days, practice's prior to theory." "The age of theory is over ..." "... absolutes ..." "... so there's only what I do at any moment." "Pleasure. Even Baudrillard in his new book ..." "He's a semiotician and dead." "Not anymore ... says our language is meaningless, for meaning— any signs—are the makings of the ruling class." "But he's still using meaningful signs to say this." "Oh, the black plague. Is it good?" "I've read all about plagues." Kiss. We don't stop kissing each other now. Your physical touch is incredibly gentle. But I can't physically feel anything 'cause I've been through a six-week relationship at the end of which the man kicked me out as fast as possible 'cause he decided he didn't know what he wanted. I must be shy of getting hurt. I think you're intelligent and lovely. Your face is keeping changing its shape. Maybe I'm hallucinating? It's not possible I can feel again after a winter and spring of no sexual love then for the second time in five years I moved in with some-body. That failed violently, forcibly.

4. The Mystery

"How, exactly, does my body feel pleasure?:

"I'm remembering fucking Eddie: I'm remembering situations of power. This's the way he likes to be fucked best: I'm on top of him. My arms reach straight to the pillow on either side of his black head. My legs slide from a sitting position straight down inside his legs so that my inner thighs nearest my cunt're rubbing his cock and so that I rising up and down am fucking his cock with my cunt. As I do this I think to myself that he likes this position more than I do. I don't come as easily in this position as when my legs're sitting on top of him because I have to be accurately acutely aware of his reaction to make sure his cock stays in my cunt and, I can't let myself fully go. I reach over Peter so my mouth is on his nipple. Or my wet tongue is flicking his nipple tip. This makes me excited more subtly than when I'm being touched: I don't come as much as violently, but I'm sort of coming all the time. I'm sort of coming all the time. Other times I stick my right hand's third finger into Eddie's asshole. It easily enters. He bucks and looks at me with surprise and openness unusual for him. Openness makes me open. My finger is reaching up and toward his cock. That opening. As his thighs're reaching up for me. Sometimes I coldly turn him over, spread the asscheeks, stick my tongue into his asshole. I don't mind doing this though I usually mind doing this on men. When I do this he groans very loudly so I know he's receiving tons of pleasure. Peter's asshole's too tight for my finger to wiggle up and I don't want to force anyone to do sexually what they don't seem to want to do. When I once mentioned, innocently?, that I had a whip back in New York and he said 'I'll have to try it,' I was surprised and thought maybe it's a go between us.

"Peter's sexually scared for instance he never comes with me 'cause he's trying not to be in love with me 'cause he loves his wife or 'cause maybe he doesn't want to come. Whenever Eddie comes, I instantaneously come he usually turns me over I've been fucking him. He's on top of me. Now I remember. My legs clasp his waist and touch each other because he likes this. I can't come in this position. Legs open up so feet rest on outer sides of ass. Rubbing bone above clit against cock-bone. Come. So as he about to come he almost stop moving. First my arms have to curl around his neck as tight as possible clasp each other. Soon as he about to come; now now, almost no movement. I'm not going to come even though I've come. Soon as he starts to come and there's almost no movement, I automatically come."

"How, exactly, does my body feel pleasure?" The girl's telling the other girl about her former lovers.

"No no. I can't talk about anything directly."

"There's a definite difference in my physical being or body between when I'm being fucked and I'm not being fucked. How can I say anything when I'm totally uncentralized or not being fucked."

"There's no sex anymore. I'm not going to have any sex. I'm not going to open up. This is me: the image. A man's suit. Look at me. I'm a woman who looks like a delicate boy and I'll never change. You can't touch me. I'm impervious. This's the way I'm happy. I'm totally elegant."

"You're out of your mind."

"Better than being laid, then sticking razor blades through my wrists."

"Living isn't so black."

"Living is a present. I'll never say otherwise. I wish I was together enough to say or do something."

"Touch me. An open quivering clit. The little red animal wiggles."

"Art, since its very beginning in prehistoric caves, has been, in our present ways of speaking, conservative."

"Art's more interesting than sex . . ."

"More rewarding. We ARE getting old," the fourteen-year-old says. "At least art doesn't end up with razor blades stuck in the wrists."

". . . only according to the art critics and they only lie about dead artists."

"I've lied down for enough artists 'cause I prefer men who hurt to men who want to own me."

"No one sexually owns another person. That's the province of art. Provenance. Roman art made dumb Roman politicians into gods. Christian art justified or rationalized the controller belief system. So what's my sexuality apart from all that's been shown me?" The other girls throw up their hands in disgust.

"Then who's responsible for the human violence in this world? Those who make. The artists."

"Who's this person I'm fucking?"

"If I'm just reflecting, I don't know. When I'm making love with you, my loving is seeing your face. The only thing I'm seeing my only identity is you."

5. Deep Female Sexuality: Marriage or Time

"When Eddie was kicking me out of his house, I put a razor blade into my right wrist in order to stop Eddie from saying 'You don't know how to love. No man will ever love you.' The people who saved me from death're my friends.

"Two men are fighting each other with cudgels. They're standing knee-deep in water. There's an overwhelming monster whose waist and hips are so soft, he looks like a woman. His right arm doesn't look like an arm. The man is puking against my building's corner wall. He doesn't flinch as I watch him. A man as he's facing out from this wall masturbates. He has a typical grin across his ugly face. I have to tell you how I get sexual pleasure. The women, rather than turning away from him, look at his exposed cock and laugh. Toward the point of death.

"Therefore I love you. Knowing that in the face of about to touch absolute darkness, there is the one rescuing that happens between two people and in the face of full knowledge. Of not only pain and incomprehendable evil and death: The real knowledge is that I want this I want to die. Horror! Knowing this—what're our jealousies our endless sexual maneuverings our social deviousnesses compared to this: we know what love is?

"What's the function of darkness? Of being ignorant?

"You said, 'Light light. Those who survive must learn mathematics.' For me there's just love, I'm scared of love. I run away from an immediacy.

"One of my legs is extending outwards. You're owning me. A sky of hot nude pearl until . . . crickets in these sheltered places . . . the wind ransacks the great planes. You are taking over control so I can relax. I'm alone on an island. I'm all by myself. Here, I'm waiting for what is to follow my collapsed dreams. I'll be more precise: I'm waiting for you 'cause I can't know anything and everything's whirling. His hand put itself on top of the clitoris and pressed. It didn't move. Her own hand was resting on her clitoris. His hand pressed down, through her hand, on the clitoris.

"I'm alone again . . . on this island. I've my books around me. I don't know why I feel lonely. This is my life, if you put it that way. You know what I mean. My life has been hard. I'm not easy and I've been, probably, irreparably, scarred. People say that someone who lives like me, in this much nothing, is sick. I'm at ease.

"You're owning me. You've touched me and I'm scared because I've decided to love you so now I'm trying to break this ownership: I phone you you're a malicious beast: I know in the past years and now you fuck lots of women and tell them you love them madly. You can't love everybody madly (I do). You're doing the same thing with me. I can't mean anything to you. I'm not special. You're shitting on my face. I hate you. I don't want to need you because I already, probably most, probably one-twentieth of me, is needing you. So after I yell at you for being as sexually romantic as I am, the next day I tell you 'I love you' when you don't want emotion. I want to die and not have responsibility.

"'I'm only interested in my abstract thought.' But what do you and I do, not so much with our bodies, but with our needs? I remember waking up. First, I see your head. I see your eyes're open and you're looking at me. I have to smile because your obvious love for me makes me smile. My thumb and second finger of my left hand hold between them your nipple, my bones. Your right hand's fingers're on my left nipple and my right hand's fingers're on your left nipple. My right hand's fingers're pulling back the extra skin of your cock tip and your lips're contorted from the scream that's coming out of your mouth, as your head turns right as I lift my body so that your cock finally hard is entering my cunt and you have to scream I remember waking."

The women are shaving their heads.

13. Introduction to Boxcar Bertha

In 1894 General Jacob S. Coxey led the famous Coxey Army March into Washington, D.C, and soon after that Dr. James Eads How, the Millionaire Hobo, organized hobo colleges all over America. By the 1930s, according to Boxcar Bertha, there were between five hundred thousand and two million hoboes in the United States, at least a tenth of whom were women. Hoboes: unattached men and women who were looking for work. Bums, on the other hand, were addicted to drugs and drink.

Men and women became hoboes for all sorts of reasons: desire to travel and have adventures, escape from bourgeois rules, but most of all, because of the lack of jobs. A hobo, living a precarious existence, hated the society through which he or she could travel, but which he or she could not, ever, flee. Nowhere to run in huge America. "To hell with such a society," Andrew Nelson said to Boxcar as they both looked at statistics on criminals, prostitutes, and hoboes. "We must somehow, destroy it, if we have to be thieves, crooks, weaklings and slaves just to exist!"

"Who can remain quiet and peace-loving and be content just to vote?" Nelson continued. "Even now in these deadly days of depression, all we have out of the chaos is the rich growing richer and more powerful and more arrogant and the bulk of the poor growing more submissive and adapting themselves by force to a lower scale of living." What is happening in the United States in 1988?

"The only hope I see left," Nelson continued, "is the refusal of the transient type to take what is given them. You and your kind are the only ones left with a real sense of freedom in America." Yesterday, hoboes; today, the most anarchist or hard-core of the rock'n'roll bands.

Boxcar Bertha's maternal grandfather was Moses Thompson, an abolitionist who worked with John Brown. He was also one of the earliest proponents in the USA of emancipation for women: of platforms such as free love, freedom from marriage, and birth control.

Abolitionism; feminism; utopianism; vegetarianism; etc. The secret history of the United States, the one that doesn't get into the children's history books, is that of populism. In Europe the left, historically, has centered around parties, for instance the Communist Party in France or the Labour Party in England. Such centralization has never existed in the United States. Rather, various movements, loosely allied to each other, have and still form what is known in the USA as the left, the underground, alternative society. Decentralization at its best and worst. The real American "melting pot."

The platforms of both feminism and of free-love are still part of this melting pot.

If Boxcar Bertha's autobiography is a story of hoboes, it is also a story of women, especially of lower-class women and of women who do not wish to be bourgeois. " . . . I found that a great army of women had taken to the road, young women mostly, gay, gallant, sure that their sex would win them a way about, far too discontented to settle down in any one place. Their stories were very much the same—no work, a whole family on relief, no prospects of marriage, the need for a lark, the need for freedom of sex and of living, and the great urge to know what other women were doing."

When Bertha, still a child, meets a woman hobo for the first time, she, Bertha, loses a virginity. The woman hobo represents freedom to this child: "I saw ... [her] ... flip a freight that had stopped at our switch to take on an empty, and ride the rods right out of our camp, waving to mother in our doorway and to the gang who held up their shovels in astonishment ... She had a book along. She had been in Detroit. She spoke of a child in Memphis. She was going to talk at an IWW meeting on the coast." Books plus travel plus free sexual choice plus hatred of capitalism are the fairytale formula for this child. "But the look on her face as she talked about going west, and the sureness with which she swung under the freight car, set my childish mind in a fever. The world was easy, like that. Even to women. It had never occurred to me before."

Feminism equals *free love*. Or does it? For the child, a woman is anyone but victim.

Boxcar begins to question the free love/freedom equation when she meets her father, Walker C. Smith, for the first time.

Walker C. Smith runs a small radical bookstore in New York City and is an anarchist both politically and personally. When Boxcar asks him how he feels about having abandoned her when she was a child, he replies that all men are her fathers and brothers, all children her sons and daughters.

"I agreed," Boxcar says cathartically, "with so much that my father said, yet he, and his thoughts, and the way he lived, left me feeling confused and helpless. I could not accept his complete lack of responsibility toward his women and his offspring, or his complete impersonality."

ODE TO OUR FATHERS WITH FULL KNOWLEDGE THAT THE TIME OF THEIR POLITICAL AND SOCIAL CONTROL IS ALMOST OVER.

I recently met a poet, quite a bit older than me, whose writings I have read for many years. We fell in love; well, I did. I learned that he's married and has several other girlfriends. At the same time he was directly affectionate to me to the point of strong emotion. I said to me that it is easy for some people to touch and be touched.

Perhaps disassociation has something to do with responsibility, that is, with the lack of it: What is felt at one moment has nothing to do with what is felt the next moment or any other moment. Lack of memory; disassociation almost in time, of moment from moment. Those who control, own, rule control best when they don't sympathize, when they disassociate. What would happen if President Reagan empathized with the Chicanos in Los Angeles? Or if he remembered his left-wing past?

Boxcar was curious: she wanted to learn about other people. She learned through a sort of dangerous journalism, by doing what those people, women, about whom she was interested, did. At a certain point she became a whore: "I'm going to learn why women let their feelings make slaves of them."

Before she had become a whore, Bertha said that she had noted that women hoboes considered their own bodies their working capital.

The same could be and has been said about women who marry. Only attributes such as class and money in this case come into consideration.

Though the hookers Bertha first meets make good money, they're always broke. For this money goes from a man, the John, to a man, the pimp. The whore, the woman, is a conduit for money. Not because of what she does—fucking doesn't equal female degradation despite the allegations of the Moral Majority. This woman is a conduit because our society is sexist, because our society has separated physical sex and feeling. Money is both the symbol and the reality of our disassociation.

The answer to the question "Why do women whore?" is, on the whole, "in order to survive." Survive economically. But most whores give their money to pimps. Bertha didn't ask why women whore; she asked why they gave their money to pimps. This question is equivalent to the question "Why do women agree to and even aggravate their own victimization?"

This question has to be answered if women are to do more than just survive.

Marie gives her money to a pimp because she likes "to wake up

in the morning with someone who was lower than she was."
Lorraine's pimp protects her. The world, a male-controlled world,
is out to get her—arrest her, make her sick, beat her up. This one
man protects her by taking her money. Spirals of victimization
swirl around and into each other.

Though she knows that pimps are scum, Boxcar has to know, to
do, so she takes on a pimp. Bill. An apt pun. Her attraction to Bill
seems to come partly from curiosity and very strongly out of sexual
satisfaction. But this attraction turns into repulsion as soon as she
realizes that Bill doesn't love her, isn't "her man." So she says to
Bill, "I wonder why pimps with so much charm and power to
thrill women use it only to degrade them and themselves."

On the left, and on the right, and in the middle and everywhere,
men have used women's sexualities and sexual needs and desires
in order to control women. For until recently a woman's work was
her sexuality: motherhood or prostitution. Though, for women,
work equaled sexuality and almost identity, female work was
regarded as second-rate, for instance, housework, and female
sexuality regarded the opposite of virginal: vicious and evil. One
result of this historical situation is that heterosexual women find
themselves in a double-bind: If they want to fight sexism, they
must deny their own sexualities. At the same time, feminism cannot
be about the denial of any female sexuality.

Nowhere to run. Nowhere to hide, but, like Marguerite Duras's
Lol Stein, in the lack of self. Or, like Boxcar, keep on travelin',
Girl.

In *Living My Life*, her autobiography, Emma Goldman tells
how, when she was fifteen years old in St. Petersburg, she met a
clerk. He courted her for several months. One day he asked her to
the hotel in which he was working. There, he grabbed her, and
raped her. "Strange, I felt no shame—only a great shock at the
discovery that the contact between man and woman could be so
brutal and so painful. I walked out in a daze, bruised in every
nerve.

"I have always felt," Goldman continued, "between two fires
in the presence of men. Their lure remained strong, but it was

always mingled with violent revulsion." [*Living My Life*, Dover, Inc., 1970, p. 23].

At another point in her autobiography Goldman describes her meeting with a brewer in Cincinnati. The unnamed man tells Emma that he's heard that she's the "greatest champion of free love" in the United States. Since he, too, believes in free love, would she, please, make love with him? Though he's a married man with grown children, he knows she believes in free love.

This " . . . respectable pillar of society," Goldman muses, "to whom free love is only a means for clandestine affairs. . . . A sense of futility came over me and of dismal isolation." [*Living My Life*, p. 197].

Both Boxcar and Emma Goldman recognized that men control women partly through their sexualities, and both loved men sexually. "Free love," for both women, was a complicated matter: "free love," or more aptly, "free sexual choice," meant that women could control their own bodies, emotions, thoughts, and lives and could choose freely sexually without being damaged beyond the usual wear-and-tear in the sexual arena. In a society which was and is still both sexist and capitalist (or postcapitalist), both Bertha and Goldman thought that it is difficult for a woman to choose and control her life, but not impossible.

"When women started to focus on sex as central to the oppression of women, there are two things they wanted: one was to be able to say 'no' to sex, and one was to be free to say 'yes' to sex. There were both of these strains. . . . Now, I think, those two branches of feminist thinking about sex have in some ways split off into two different hardened positions within feminism . . . and one is associated with the Women Against Pornography movement (WAP). . . . The other side is what I'll call the liberationist position, which wants to free women to explore our own sexuality, which has so long been repressed and male defined." [Shulman, Alix Kates in an interview, *Rolling Stock #10*, 1985].

This sexual bind, which both Bertha and Goldman recognized, is still one of the major definers of women's lives. In terms of this bind, the complexities of understanding of women's lives found in

Boxcar Bertha: An Autobiography renegotiate the schism between the feminists who have interiorized the "Virgin" of patriarchal religion and society into their own beliefs and those feminists who refuse to comprehend that sexuality because of sexism is a problem for most women.

Consider western patriarchal religion one last time. There are seven Christian sins: pride, anger, envy, avarice, sloth, gluttony, and lust. (I believe I've listed them correctly.) What are the sins of our high political leaders? Overwhelmingly, their collective sin is a lack of sympathy, an inability to empathize. Lack of sympathy is ignorance. Where is ignorance in the Christian negative pantheon? Boxcar Bertha felt for other humans to the extent that she had to know them, become them, a whore, homeless, willing to suffer, to learn. Such knowledge, such *human* knowledge is complex.

(This introduction is for my friend Melissa.)

1988

14.

Some American Cities

Forget that the New York City streets are literally cracking open. Forget that one prominent New York politician recently stated that it does not matter that there will be over 30,000 homeless AIDS victims on the streets next year, for all of them will soon die. All that matters are motorcycles. In Manhattan, the borough of New York City that most people mean when they say "New York City," the Hell's Angels, despisers of all Japanese bikes or "rice burners," own all motorcycle territory. Any Japanese bike that dares to sit on a New York street is liable to be mauled by a passer-by Angel; any non-Harley rider invites Angel spit and mockery. The owner of the Japanese bike, who possesses a non-American bike simply because he or she doesn't know better, cannot find a Manhatten bike mechanic willing to lower himself enough to work on "rice burners."

I finally accomplished the impossible: managed to score a mechanic who would fix the kickstand and back brake on my Honda which some Angel had kicked in.

Though I had easily shipped my Honda from London to New York (the shippers had thrown it into the crate along with the books), I couldn't learn how to register it in New York. After several trips to the Motor Vehicle Building and consultations with bored clerks who weren't sure where England might be, I gathered that I would have to bring the motorcycle through Customs a second time. This time I would pay the inspectors, my government, over two thousand dollars, more than the cost of the bike, for transformations of the exhaust and other parts from the English to the American system. Then, my motorcycle could be legal.

In Manhattan, legality is costly.

For six months I drove my motorcycle in fear of potholes ranging from two to three feet in diameter that seemed to descend into Hell, of car especially truck drivers who signaled, if at all, according to a system devised by a maniacal three-year-old, and especially of policemen. Policemen who the moment they sighted my non-American license plate wanted to know why I was unpatriotic and once beat me up in order to find out.

One day, after having held a long discussion with the members of five squad cars who had been disturbed by this lack of patriotism, I visited the mechanic to learn if he had any ideas about how my vehicle could attain legal status. I still didn't have an American license; fear of policemen was preventing me from taking the necessary tests. Legality seemed a lost affair.

The mechanic, a curly-haired wiry Italian, asked me if I'd like to light up. His garage was open on two sides to the street.

"Aren't there cops around here?" I naively inquired.

"Of course. There's a cop right over there."

I turned around and saw a tall middle-age man standing in the back of the garage.

This policeman, the mechanic, and I proceeded to smoke pot mixed with hash.

While the law officer bought three hundred dollars of pot from the mechanic, the latter showed me photos of all his cars and boats. I remember that there were six boats, the largest, according to its owner, sixty feet, and several cars and motorcycles including a Jag and a Harley-Davidson. An American bike.

"Last night," said the mechanic, "I was driving the Jag at about

140 m.p.h. A cop pulled me over. When I was reaching for my license, he saw my gun. I always carry a gun; you have to in this business. Then he really went for me. When he finally looks at my I.D., he sees this detective's badge."

In New York City, detective badges are pure gold.

"'Sorry, sir,' says the policeman saluting. 'I had no way of knowing.'

"'Well, don't do it again,' I said.

"We both drove on at about 140 m.p.h."

The mechanic then showed me six detective badges. He handled the cars for several police precincts, he explained to me, and the police, in return, had given him several presents.

I wondered what happened to all the drugs that cops had confiscated.

Perhaps New York City isn't disintegrating. Perhaps one system, that order based on a certain kind of capitalism, is disintegrating while another world, one of tribes, criminal and other, anarchic, is rising out of the rotting streets, sidewalks, and bridges.

In the United States, the death of urban order is no new story. When I was in Detroit, I was informed that it was dangerous to walk unaccompanied from one's car to the grocery store. In Detroit, deserted car factories, broken glass windows, rose up from streets covered by snow. One grand hotel, perhaps the grandest of its kind, long deserted, had a bum living in one of its topmost suites. Below, wild dogs and wild cats roamed through the snow. A sign, I was told, of a rotting city.

In 1968, San Francisco was "the city of love." Two years later, media attention and a turn from soft to hard drugs had transformed the early hippy scene, located in the Haight-Ashbery section of town, into one of waste and death.

The city quickly revived: by 1974 the old hippy scene was now, what the media named for lack of a better word, "gay." We called it, "beyond the third sex." None but businessmen thought that there was any division between "gay" and "straight," for the real straights lived in the business section of the city never visited by those whose main goal in life was to have fun.

One magazine, obviously a "straight" one, trying to list all the gay bars in town, listed every bar outside the business sections.

Despite the gentrification promoted by the recent Mayor Feinstein, the city's culture has remained gay. I use "gay" for lack of a better word. Despite sexual inclinations, most San Franciscans partake of this gay lifestyle.

San Franciscans have two jokes. The first is that the United States government for years has encouraged all the freaks to move to this city so that the earthquake will destroy all of us. Second: however wierd a person thinks himself or herself, that person will always find someone wierder in San Francisco. Here tattoos are as common as rednecks in Georgia; in the past year, two new piercing shops have opened.

In the face of growing national recession, San Francisco is not decaying. Crime and homelessness are on a slight rise; on the other hand, the community has been and is positively dealing with the problems of AIDS, with government censorship, and with the lack of governmental funding. Perhaps partly due to lack of connection to the New York and international art markets, art and writing, especially in underground forms, are thriving in this city.

San Franciscans tend to be more than provincial: they justifiably regard their culture as an oasis in conservative-to-radical-right-wing America. It could be that this provincialism, a lack of connection to corporate markets such as the New York art and publishing worlds, and a gay lifestyle are enabling San Francisco, for the moment, to combat the decay engendered by American postcapitalism and imperialism.

15. The Meaning of the Eighties

NYC

1981

Dear Lin—

Today my mother met William Burroughs. She got, she said, invited to this dinner party which was all men. As the token woman. She said William Burroughs has the intelligence of the sharpest knife she's ever met. She stood against one of the dining room walls and watched him go to work. He likes animals. She didn't want to talk to him; she wanted to be invisible and watch. My mother wants to be a wall.

P.S. I'm not going to ever have anything to do with anyone.

HERE ARE LETTERS BETWEEN TWO SEVEN-YEAR-OLD GIRLS ABOUT THE EIGHTIES. THEIR NAMES ARE ZOOZOO AND LINDA AND THEY HAVE PARENTS.

SF, near the Mission

Dear Zoozoo,

Life's fine even though yesterday I got attacked by a bicycle gang. Seven black kids, they weren't fucking older than me but they were fucking bigger, rode around me on their bicycles and they said that since I was a lezzy and a punk, they were going to kill me. I was lucky because they weren't going to kill me now. I guess that's why I'm alive.

Mom told me not to be upset about this NAUSEATING incident because the problem is political, not personal. She said I mustn't ever mistake the political for the personal or else I'll be selfish. "Better off selfish than dead," I know my father'd say, but I have no idea who he is. SHE said that the Mayor in her (can a Mayor be a her?) effort to get rid of Chicanos and gays is rezoning the city so that the gays have to move into the Mission, the Chicano territory. The Chicanos, who have a good form of machismo, have arms or are up in arms and are setting gay hangouts like "Rush" factories on fire.

I'm a child and I don't need this shit. I told mom I need education. She said she was now hanging out with these guys who do *Research* (magazine), they used to do *Search and Destroy!* and these people know about all and the only things that are interesting here. Like about Mark Pauline's computer-run monsters who attack gigantic photos of the Virgin Mary and someone named Reagan; like about real artists, artists of the body, tattooists. If I really want to learn, I could go out like her and find where learning is, rather than complain all the time. She said that if I think the system's going to help me, I'm already dead. My mother's too tough.

1984

SF

Dear Zooz—

I'm sick of your NYC punk. Here's where the real violence is. Down in San Diego, the Chicanos are sniping at cars on the freeways. The Chicanos live in these tracks or gullies on the hills above the freeways. They don't REALLY live in gullies; rather they sneak over the Tijuana border and squat in gullies until they can earn the under-minimum-wage pittances the rich whites hand out for services such as MAID and gardener. But this is a lot of money in Mexico where their extended families are living. Chicanos have to have fun too; for fun, they set empty lots on fire and snipe at freeway cars. I'd do the same thing if I could, but you don't understand violence.

That is 'cause you don't understand real art 'cause your NYC art world eats money.

And as my father, who would say anything 'cause I've never met him, says, money isn't where it's at.

Speaking of violence which I love madly except when it's against me, I'm reading this writer William Gibson who's in some ways better than William Burroughs and in some ways, not. Read him, fuckface. "The sky above the port was the color of television, tuned to a dead channel, and a dead cock was coming out of it." He's the first writer I've read in a long time who talks about you and me. I'm going to be a writer. As soon as I learn to write. The ways I want to write. (Mom said it's going to be hard for me to be a writer 'cause I'm a girl. She should know.)

NYC

Dear Linda,

I'm using your full name because if you want to be a writer, you're going to have to get rid of all that counterculture crap which is just provincial. San Franciscans are isolated. Mother says that if you want to be an artist whose work matters, you both have to be part of the large world and affect the large world. You can't affect the large world if you're using some wierd language you and your friends invented and you wear clothes so full of holes, your tits show. It's not your violence I object to. It's the provincialism and isolation that underlie violence. You have to stop seeing only your side of things because your side of things is a gutter and you're going to live in the gutter and never be a writer if you go on as you are going. Writers *communicate;* they are not autistic and everyone knows that the only reason people stay in San Francisco is because they're mad.

What artists (I hate how you always use "real") are now doing is repeating other points-of-view. Objects. We have to enter the world. And we have to make money. I've seen mother fuck with poverty and it almost killed her art. (Sex isn't worth it.) Maybe you don't see enough bums. Every day I see at least a hundred bums in the street. Maybe you don't know what real violence is. Real violence is poverty and it does nothing but stink and so the art that comes out of it stinks too.

The artists here, including mother (father went off with some rich dealer, but he never mattered) utilize mirroring techniques. They simply re-represent various parts of the culture. With none of that hippy moralism that sent our parents raging into punk; without the stylistic pyrotechnics—prettiness—your William Gibson wears like a pink dress. Only drag queens are allowed to be pretty. Here's literature, by a guy named Richard Prince, who's principally an artist but can make anything:

> He could never imagine what it must be like to spend an entire day without ever having to avoid a mirror. And where he lived, he made sure, never had a reflection, and any surface that did so, got dulled or rubbed out, and any surface that became stubborn and kept its polish, got thrown in a bucket.
> Clean.

1986
London

Dear Zoozoozoo,

Fuck you darling, mother and I are in London. New Yorkers, my dear, are so provincial; they live in that death that is New York and never know there's a whole world outside their island culture.

The GLC (Greater London Council) (Americans are so vulgar and stupid one has to explain the simplest things to them) runs this city. Londoners enjoy mugging-free clean tubes (subways), excellent and free medical services, and often live in government-financed lesbian communes. Everything here is fun! Every night I go to this club *TABOO* and a big, gay beauty who's actually American! throws me around and everyone takes off some or all clothes. Rachel Auburn, the club's DJ, who also designs clothes, usually wears a tutu and gold pasties. Everyone's bi and no one fucks.

They do other things. That's the English way. Style. At five o'clock in the morning, we all go home. I'm stylish now and I'm never going to suffer again.

Mother says that life here is good for women only because feminism is so strong. But the English feminists are strange because they believe that a woman has to be a lesbian to be a feminist and to be lesbian is not to sleep with other women, as back home, but not to want to sleep with men. Since many of the lesbians here aren't doctrinaire feminists, most of the feminists don't have sex. Mother isn't having as much fun as me, but when I'm an old woman, I'm going to be an eccentric so I can have lots of fun. Because I'm going to be a writer, and if you don't have fun, you can't write well. Americans don't understand.

As for art. Art as in *ARTFORUM*. Really. Everyone here, I mean everyone on the streets, communicates through music, tattoos, and clothes. All of us'd do anything for Jean-Paul Gaultier. None of us earns money. So who needs New York City art, the Mary Boone stock market game?

NYC

Dear Lin,

Mom and I do what we can. We keep all the Levelors closed so that no light enters the apartment. Mom doesn't want any lover to penetrate her territory more than three times and I never want to be touched. I don't give a damn whether or not you understand. Mom is a famous artist and beginning to make money. They say that the eighties is about emptiness. But. This is real style.

1989

London

Dear Zoozoo,

I've watched a country go to hell in four years. It's probably taken longer than that: when I first came over here, I was so

American, I couldn't understand that I was living in a foreign culture. Much less that the culture was almost dead. Perhaps due to a triple multiplication: a class system times a woman named Margaret Thatcher times a longing for both the days of the Empire and for nineteenth-century trade unionism.

I've seen about half of our friends go out on drugs or die from AIDS. Now I've watched a nation die. I've seen how, when a political-economic structure turns from civilized social welfare to a poor imitation of American postcapitalism, every single person's life radically changes. The rich and successful here are basking in their form of death or boredom. The others, like James Dean in *Rebel Without a Cause*, an American film, would go anywhere if they had anywhere to go.

I want *out* now. I don't know what to do with my life, but I won't live in this death.

P.S. That stupid wall which anyone could have gotten over is down: the whole world has changed.

NYC

Dear Lin,

Come here! Because the idiots in our government tried to pass a censorship bill, and perhaps will, all the artists who, I agree with you, are provincial and egotistic in their provinciality, finally outraged, are battling. Now the city is a lot of radical and good art and homeless occupying the parks and sidewalks and pipes rising like snakes up through pavements and buildings. Makes William Gibson into an outmoded writer. While this city's decaying, artists and blacks and even others are fighting back. Minimalism's gone to hell. The blacks're leading our way. So get your ass over here. We might as well go to battle for joy as hard as we can because whether we fight or we elect to live like zombies, we have to die anyway.

Get your hot pussy here, girl.

1990

16. | Bodies of Work

Against Ordinary Language: The Language of the Body

Preface Diary

I have now been bodybuilding for ten years, seriously for almost five years.

During the past few years, I have been trying to write about bodybuilding.

Having failed time and time again, upon being offered the opportunity to write this essay, I made the following plan: I would attend the gym as usual. Immediately after each workout, I would describe all I had just experienced, thought, and done. Such diary descriptions would provide the raw material.

After each workout, I forgot to write. Repeatedly. I . . . some part of me . . . the part of the "I" who bodybuilds . . . was rejecting language, any verbal description of the processes of bodybuilding.

I shall begin describing, writing about bodybuilding in the only way that I can: I shall begin by analyzing this rejection of ordinary or verbal language. What is the picture of the antagonism between bodybuilding and verbal language?

A Language Which is Speechless

Imagine that you are in a foreign country. Since you are going to be in this place for some time, you are trying to learn the language. At the point of commencing to learn the new language, just before having started to understand anything, you begin forgetting your own. Within strangeness, you find yourself without a language.

It is here, in this geography of no language, this negative space, that I can start to describe bodybuilding. For I am describing that which rejects language.

Elias Canetti, who grew up within a multitude of spoken languages, began his autobiography by recounting a memory. In this, his earliest remembrance, the loss of language is threatened: "My earliest memory is dipped in red. I come out of a door on the arm of a maid, the door in front of me is red, and to the left a staircase goes down, equally red . . ." A smiling man walks up to the child; the child, upon request, sticks out his tongue whereupon the man flips open a jackknife and holds the sharp blade against the red tongue.

". . . He says: 'Now we'll cut off his tongue.'"

At the last moment, the man pulls the knife back.

According to memory, this sequence happens every day. "That's how the day starts," Canetti adds, "and it happens very often."[1]

I am in the gym every three of four days. What happens there? What does language in that place look like?

According to cliché, athletes are stupid. Meaning: they are inarticulate. The spoken language of bodybuilders makes this cliché real. The verbal language in the gym is minimal and almost senseless, reduced to numbers and a few nouns. "Sets," "squats," "reps" . . . The only verbs are "do" or "fail", adjectives and adverbs no longer exist; sentences, if they are at all, are simple.

This spoken language is kin to the "language games" Wittgenstein proposes in his *The Brown Book*.[2]

In a gym, verbal language or language whose purpose is meaning occurs, if at all, only at the edge of its becoming lost.

But when I am in the gym, my experience is that I am immersed in a complex and rich world.

What actually takes place when I bodybuild?

The crossing of the threshold from the world defined by verbal language into the gym in which the outside world is not allowed (and all of its languages) (in this sense, the gym is sacred) takes several minutes. What happens during these minutes is that I forget. Masses of swirling thought, verbalized insofar as I am conscious of them, disappear as mind or thought begins to focus.

In order to analyze this focusing, I must first describe bodybuilding in terms of intentionality.

Bodybuilding is a process, perhaps a sport, by which a person shapes her or his own body. This shaping is always related to the growth of muscular mass.

During aerobic and circuit training, the heart and lungs are exercised. But muscles will grow only if they are not exercised or moved, but actually broken down. The general law behind bodybuilding is that muscle, if broken down in a controlled fashion and then provided with the proper growth factors such as nutrients and rest, will grow back larger than before.

In order to break down specific areas of muscles, whatever areas one wants to enlarge, it is necessary to work these areas in isolation up to failure.

Bodybuilding can be seen to be about nothing but *failure*. A bodybuilder is always working around failure. Either I work an isolated muscle mass, for instance one of the tricep heads, up to failure. In order to do this, I exert the muscle group almost until the point that it can no longer move.

But if I work the same muscle group to the point that it can no longer move, I must move it through failure. I am then doing what are named "negative reps," working the muscle group beyond its power to move. Here is the second method of working with failure.

Whatever way I choose, I always want to work my muscle, muscular group, until it can no longer move: I want to fail. As soon as I can accomplish a certain task, so much weight for so many reps during a certain time span, I must always increase one aspect of this equation, weights reps or intensity, so that I can again come to failure.

I want to break muscle so that it can grow back larger, but I do not want to destroy muscle so that growth is prevented. In order to avoid injury, I first warm up the muscular group, then carefully bring it up to failure. I do this by working the muscular group through a calculated number of sets during a calculated time span. If I tried immediately to bring a muscle group up to failure by lifting the heaviest weight I could handle, I might injure myself.

I want to shock my body into growth; I do not want to hurt it.

Therefore, in bodybuilding, *failure* is always connected to counting. I calculate which weight to use; I then count off how many times I lift that weight and the seconds between each lift. This is how I control the intensity of my workout.

Intensity times movement of maximum weight equals muscular destructions (muscular growth).

Is the equation between destruction and growth also a formula for art?

Bodybuilding is about failure because bodybuilding, body growth and shaping, occurs in the face of the material, of the body's inexorable movement toward its final failure, toward death.

To break down a muscle group, I want to make that group work up to, even beyond, capacity. To do this, it helps and even is necessary to visualize the part of the body that is involved. Mind or thought, then, while bodybuilding, is always focused on number or counting and often on precise visualizations.

Certain bodybuilders have said that bodybuilding is a form of meditation.

What do I do when I bodybuild? I visualize and I count. I estimate weight; I count sets; I count repetitions; I count seconds between repetitions; I count time, seconds or minutes, between sets: From the beginning to the end of each workout, in order to maintain intensity, I must continually count.

For this reason, a bodybuilder's language is reduced to a minimal, even a closed, set of nouns and to numerical repetition, to one of the simplest of language games.

Let us name this language game, *the language of the body.*

The Richness of the Language of the Body

In order to examine such a language, a language game which resists ordinary language, through the lens of ordinary language or language whose tendency is to generate syntax or to make meanings proliferate, I must use an indirect route.

In another of his books, Elias Canetti begins talking from and about that geography that is without verbal language:

> *A marvelously luminous, viscid substance is left behind in me, defying words . . .*
> *A dream: a man who unlearns the world's languages until nowhere on earth does he understand what people are saying.*[3]

Being in Marrakesh is Canetti's dream made actual. There are languages here, he says, but I understand none of them. The closer I am moving towards foreignness, into strangeness, toward understanding foreignness and strangeness, the more I am losing my own language. The small loss of language occurs when I journey to and into my own body. Is my body a foreign land to me? What is this picture of "my body" and "I"? For years, I said in the beginning of this essay, I have wanted to describe bodybuilding; whenever I tried to do so, ordinary language fled from me.

"Man," Heidegger says, "is the strangest."[4] Why? Because everywhere he or she belongs to being or to strangeness or chaos, and yet everywhere he or she attempts to carve a path through chaos:

> *Everywhere man makes himself a path; he ventures into all realms of the essent, of the overpowering power, and in so doing he is flung out of all paths.*[5]

The physical or material, that which is, is constantly and unpredictably changing: it is chaotic. This chaos twines around death. For it is death that rejects all of our paths, all of our meanings.

Whenever anyone bodybuilds, he or she is always trying to understand and control the physical in the face of this death. No wonder bodybuilding is centered around failure.

The antithesis between meaning and essence has often been noted. Wittgenstein at the end of the *Tractatus*:

> *The sense of the world must lie outside the world. In the world everything is as it is, and everything happens as it does happen—in it no values exist, and if they did, they'd have no value.*
> *For all that happens and is the case is accidental.*[6]

If ordinary language or meanings lie outside essence, what is the position of that language game which I have named *the language of the body*? For bodybuilding (a language of the body) rejects ordinary language and yet itself constitutes a language, a method for understanding and controlling the physical which in this case is also the self.

I can now directly talk about bodybuilding. (As if speech is ever direct.)

The language game named *the language of the body* is not arbitrary. When a bodybuilder is counting, he or she is counting his or her own breath.

Canetti speaks of the beggars of Marrakesh who possess a similar and even simpler language game: they repeat the name of God.

In ordinary language, meaning is contextual. Whereas the cry of the beggar means nothing other than what it is; in the city of the beggar, the impossible (as the Wittgenstein of the *Tractatus* and Heidegger see it) occurs in that meaning and breath become one.

Here is the language of the body; here, perhaps, is the reason why bodybuilders experience bodybuilding as a form of meditation.

"I understood the seduction there is in a life that reduces everything to the simplest kind of repetition,"[7] Canetti says. A life in which meaning and essence no longer oppose each other. A life of meditation.

"I understood what those blind beggars really are: the saints of repetition . . ."[8]

The Repetition of the One: The Glimpse Into Chaos or Essence

I am in the gym. I am beginning to work out. I either say the name "bench press," then walk over to it, or simply walk over to it. Then, I might picture the number of my first weight; I probably, since I usually begin with the same warm-up weight, just place the appropriate weights on the bar. Lifting this bar off its rests, then down to my lower chest, I count "1." I am visualizing this bar, making sure it touches my chest at the right spot, placing it back on its rests. "2." I repeat the same exact motions. "3." . . . After twelve repetitions, I count off thirty seconds while increasing my weights. "1." . . . The identical process begins again only this time I finish at "10." . . . All these repetitions end only when I finish my workout.

On counting: Each number equals one inhalation and one exhalation. If I stop my counting or in any other way lose focus, I risk dropping or otherwise mishandling a weight and so damaging my body.

In this world of the continual repetition of a minimal number of elements, in this aural labyrinth, it is easy to lose one's way. When all is repetition rather than the production of meaning, every path resembles every other path.

Every day, in the gym, I repeat the same controlled gestures with the same weights, the same reps, . . . the same breath patterns. But now and then, wandering within the labyrinths of my body, I come upon something. Something I can know because knowledge depends on difference. An unexpected event. For though I am only repeating certain gestures during certain time spans, my body, being material, is never the same; my body is controlled by change and by chance.

For instance, yesterday, I worked chest. Usually I easily

benchpress the bar plus sixty pounds for six reps. Yesterday, unexpectedly, I barely managed to lift this weight at the sixth rep. I looked for a reason. Sleep? Diet? Both were usual. Emotional or work stress? No more than usual. The weather? Not good enough. My unexpected failure at the sixth rep was allowing me to see, as if through a window, not to any outside, but inside my own body, to its workings. I was being permitted to glimpse the laws that control my body, those of change or chance, laws that are barely, if at all, knowable.

By trying to control, to shape, my body through the calculated tools and methods of bodybuilding, and time and again, in following these methods, failing to do so, I am able to meet that which cannot be finally controlled and known: the body.

In this meeting lies the fascination, if not the purpose, of bodybuilding. To come face to face with chaos, with my own failure or a form of death.

Canetti describes the architecture of a typical house in the geographical labyrinth of Marrakesh. The house's insides are cool, dark. Few, if any, windows look out into the street. For the entire construction of this house, windows, etc., is directed inward, to the central courtyard where only openness to the sun exists.

Such an architecture is a mirror of the body. When I reduce verbal language to minimal meaning, to repetition, I close the body's outer windows. Meaning approaches breath as I bodybuild, as I begin to move through the body's labyrinths, to meet, if only for a second, that which my consciousness ordinarily cannot see. Heidegger: "The being there of historical man means: to be posited as the breach into which the preponderant power of being bursts in its appearing, in order that this breach itself should shatter against being."[9]

In our culture, we simultaneously fetishize and disdain the athlete, a worker in the body. For we still live under the sign of Descartes. This sign is also the sign of patriarchy. As long as we continue to regard the body, that which is subject to change, chance, and death, as disgusting and inimical, so long shall we continue to regard our own selves as dangerous others.

1993

Notes
1. Elias Canetti, *The Tongue Set Free*, New York: The Seabury Press, 1979, p. 5.
2. Here and throughout the rest of this article, whenever I use the phrase "language game," I am referring to Ludwig Wittgenstein's discussion of language games in *The Brown Book*, (Wittgenstein, *The Blue and Brown Books*, New York: Harper and Row, Publishers, 1960).
3. Elias Canetti, *The Voices of Marrakesh*, New York: The Seabury Press, 1978, p. 23.
4. Martin Heidegger, *An Introduction to Metaphysics*, New York: Anchor Books, 1961, p. 12 5. By "man," Heidegger means "human."
5. Ibid., p. 127.
6. Ludwig Wittgenstein, *Tractatus Logico Philosphicus*, London: Routledge and Kegan Paul Ltd., 1972, p. 145.
7. Canetti, *The Voices of Marrakesh*, p. 25.
8. Ibid., p. 26.
9. Heidegger, *An Introduction to Metaphysics*, p. 137.

17. | Colette

1. A Memory of Childhood

I have one childhood memory concerning Colette, that writer exemplaire of childhood and of the fresh perspective, the reality of joy, we call naif or childish.

My late childhood: I was already in high school. It was the day John F. Kennedy died. Suddenly, I'm remembering that I didn't understand why, all the students and teachers around me were watching. What? A TV had been pulled into the main auditorium of the school. There all of us were sitting on chairs and watching. The majority, students and teachers, were crying. I still didn't understand, somewhat what was happening, mainly why. Unable to understand, then to bear my confusion, I ran away from the school.

My boyfriend at that time was a filmmaker and film theoretician. I couldn't tell either my parents or anyone at my school about him, for he was an artist. Artists are not acceptable boyfriends. At that time I was living a double life, a life in the parent/school world I had to inhabit and a life in the art world about which I could not talk. On the day of John F. Kennedy's assassination, I ran away to the forbidden world.

My boyfriend worked in and out of a place and community primarily of filmmakers, but also of poets, dancers, etc., called the Film Co-Op. That day, when I entered the room on lower Park Avenue, that one room which was the whole of the Co-Op, I remember a number of filmmakers including Adolphas Mekas were in that room, mourning. Not because of the assassination of JFK: that seemed to have happened in another world. They were mourning because Jean Cocteau, the French poet, playwright, filmmaker, artist, and above all friend, had just suicided, these filmmakers conjectured, over the death of his comrade Edith Piaf.

I do not know the facts: the truth of what I remember. Whether Cocteau did suicide due to Piaf's death. My memory is true: my memory of when I learned what matters. On that day, for me the child, there were two distinct worlds: the world of politicians political assassinations schools correct learning, and the world of artists. Artists were those who lived by and died from love. Cocteau Piaf Colette. I knew that, in her older years, Colette and Cocteau had been friends.

> I learned to respect Jean Cocteau before coming to love him. In those days, whenever I felt lazy, I would consider the example of this young man whose works were not frivolous yet who always worked as though for the fun of it.[1]

I made my childish connections; I made my childish myth of a reality defined by friendships and kinds of values and commitments neither my parents nor my teachers had taught nor seemed to know.

What, precisely, is this myth?

2. The Myth Of Colette: The Beginning Of The Myth

Colette's writing began in her disappearance. When he was in his thirties, Henri Gauthiers-Villars, known simply as Willy, married a twenty-year-old girl. Colette. He was already the author of a book of sonnets, one about Mark Twain, a body of music criticism, and numerous pieces of pulp fiction such as *Maîtresse d' esthétes*. Two years after the marriage he instructed his young wife to put her memories of her school days into writing, with all the spicy details, for they were short of money. Though she did as he told her to the best of her ability, Willy decided her writing was useless. Five years later he changed his mind. When he published *Claudine à l'école*, Colette's first novel, under his own name, both the novel and Willy became famous.

Luce Irigaray in *Ce Sexe qui n'en est pas un* says that according to the discourse of the (male) world, female sexuality is "lack,' 'atrophy' (of the sexual organ), and 'penis envy,' the penis being the only sexual organ of recognized value."[2] In such a world the young Colette was the perfect female author: nonexistent.

Even more significant is the implied connection of writing to sexuality, and thus to identity.

3. The Second Part of the Myth of Colette: Colette's Escape Out of (Social) Nonbeing

Sexuality is central. If it was sexuality—in this case, the discourse of marriage—which made Colette descend into nonbeing, it was her sexuality which allowed her escape.

Colette left Willy and began living alone. A month later, in order to earn her money, she started working as a mime, a kind of theatrical stripper. For the next five years her lover was Sophie-Mathilde-Adéle de Morny, Missy. At the end of Colette's *Le Pur et l'impur*, a woman who has been heterosexual says to her girlfriend her lover, "'Trust me utterly, since I now have nothing to hide from you, I feel pure, I am your ally and no longer your victim.'"[3] And Colette began writing under her own name. In the title story of *Les Vrilles de la vigne*, a collection published only two years after Colette had left Willy, a nightingale loved to sing during the day. Then a vine wrapped up her limbs, imprisoning her, imprisoning her mouth, during the sexual nighttime. The bird escapes and now sings all day and night so that she will never again be imprisoned.

Material independence, sexual freedom from men, writing as

one desires. These three are related, even interdependent. Colette's writing was the means by which she now made both money and her identity. In writing autobiographical fiction she freely created her own I/eye.

4. The Third Part of the Myth of Colette: The Double I/Eyes

Who is this "I"?

Who was Colette?

Sexuality is central. Female sexuality is not negative. "Woman 'touches herself' all the time, and moreover no one can forbid her to do so, for her genitals are formed of two lips in continuous contact. Thus, within her self, she is already two—but not divisible into one(s)—that caress each other."[4] Female sexuality not only exists, it is double: it is the toucher and the touched. Likewise, Colette's speech was double: her I/eye looked at/created her I/eye.

More precisely: who was this non-Oedipal I?

Colette wrote about her mother in order to define herself. The mother was presence while the child was absence. "I always remained in touch with the personage who, little by little, has dominated all the rest of my work: the personage of my mother . . ."[5] ". . . my felicity knew another and less commonplace secret: the presence of her who, instead of receding far from me through the gates of death, has revealed herself more vividly to me as I grow older."[6] As for the child: "Our uncanny turbulence was never accompanied by any sound . . . Our only sin, our single misdeed, was silence, and a kind of miraculous vanishing. For perfectly innocent reasons, for the sake of a liberty that no one denied us . . ."[7]

The woman who is mother and child cannot be ego-centered, one, unified. Being multiple her natural movement is to go outward, to roam. The child Colette wants to be a sailor.

Her sexuality, likewise, doesn't have the singleness of an orgasmic definition. Female sexual awakening is a process of traveling rather than of arriving coming and stopping. The woman comes, but she comes to somewhere only to go somewhere else, as in a dream. A woman's rising, sexual rising is the rising up of dreams, of writing.

For Colette, this was her sexual awakening:

> *Two arms, singularly adept at lifting a sleeping form, encircled my waist and my neck, at the same time gathering the blankets and sheets about me. My cheeks felt the colder air of the stairs, a muffled heavy step descended slowly, rocking me at each pace with a gentle motion. Did I really wake? I doubt it. Only a dream could waft a little girl right out of her childhood and place her, neither surprised nor unwilling, in the very midst of a hypocritical and adventurous adolescence. Only a dream could thus turn a loving child into the ungrateful creature that she will become tomorrow, the crafty accomplice of the stranger, the forgetful one who will leave her mother's house without a backward glance . . .[8]*

The dream, or sexuality, transforms the female identity utterly.

> *When day broke, I failed to recognize my old garret.[8]*

Such shiftings of identity, such plurality which cannot be singly named or easily defined, such ambiguous identity which cannot be "proper" became Colette's writing and language. In another story in *La Maison de Claudine* she tells how as a child she thought "presbytery" was a scientific term for a certain small yellow-and-black striped snail. When they told her that a "presbytery" was a priest's house, Colette "longed to compel Monsieur Millot (the priest), during my pleasure, to inhabit the empty shell of the little "presbytery" snail . . ."[9] Finally, rather than submitting to their rigid mono-language, Colette shut up. In her silence she created her own kingdom, THE PRESBYTERY, her multilanguage of multieverything, herself as ruler, magic female writer.

This, for me, is the myth of Colette.

1985

Notes
1. Colette, in an issue of *Empreintes*, May 1950.
2. Luce Irigaray, *Ce Sexe qui n'en est pas un*, translated by Catherine Porter, Cornell University Press, p. 23.
3. Colette, *Le Pur et l'impur*, translated by Herma Briffault, Farrar, Straus & Giroux, Inc. p. 174.
4. Irigaray, p. 24.
5. Colette, *La Maison de Claudine*, translated by Una Vincenzo Troubridge and Enid McLoed, Penguin Books, Ltd., p. 19.
6. Colette, *La Maison de Claudine*, p. 19.
7. Colette, *La Maison de Claudine*, pp. 25, 27.
8. Colette, *La Maison de Claudine*, p. 43.
9. Colette, *La Maison de Claudine*, p. 46.

18. Seeing Gender

Childhood

When I was a child, the only thing I wanted was to be a pirate. Because I wasn't a stupid child, I knew that I couldn't.

I couldn't send men down the plank, I couldn't see sights stranger and more wonderful than those seen in my childhood dreams, I couldn't dwell in seas that would freeze my lips and whose living and dead denizens would tear away my bones, I couldn't swing from any yardarm.

"Because," I announced, "my parents won't let me.

"If only my parents were dead, I could do all that I wanted to do: I could run away to sea."

I couldn't murder my parents because I couldn't imagine murdering them. There was no such thing in my world as murdering parents. And pirates weren't people who had murdered parents because pirates didn't have parents.

I was clever, like a rat, so I came up with another way that I could become a pirate. I was well aware that, in my family, my mother was the one who made all the decisions. I concluded that I wasn't a pirate because my mother wouldn't allow me to be one.

I argued: as if she's a map, she's the key to my buried treasure.

I argued: this is my mother's personality; she's a woman who loves to laugh and she never has any fun. She lives in a monogamous marriage with a man who isn't mean enough to her, who yields to her every silly whim.

I argued: if my mother begins to have an illicit affair with a handsome, intelligent, and nasty man, she'll know what it is to be happy and then she'll know that I need happiness and so I should be allowed to be a pirate.

With all my girlish strength, I begged all the dead pirates who lived in the seas to make my mother fall in love with a devastating man.

It was then that I knew that I could never be a pirate because I was a girl.

I couldn't even run away to sea like Herman Melville.

Barely born, I was dead. The world of my parents, my bossy mother and my weak father, the world in which I had to wear white gloves and panty girdles even though I was skinny, was a dead world. Whereas pirates lived in the *living* world because pirates had fun. Since pirates lived in my books, I ran into the world of books, the only living world I, a girl, could find.

I never left that world.

Adult

I'm no longer a child and I still want to be, to live with the pirates.

Because I want to live forever in wonder.

The difference between me as child and me as adult is this and only this: when I was a child, I longed to travel into, to live in wonder. Now, I know, as much as I can know anything, that to travel into wonder is to be wonder. So it matters little whether I travel by plane, by rowboat, or by book. Or, by dream.

I do not see, for there is no *I* to see. This is what the pirates know.

There is only seeing and, in order to go to see, one must be a pirate.

Looking for a body

When I was a child, I knew that the separation between me and piracy had something to do with being a girl. With gender. With being in a dead world. So gender had something to do with death. And not with sight, for *to see was to be other than dead. To see was to be an eye*, not an *I*.

But it's not enough to live in books. The older I become, the more insufficient becomes this living in books. I want to find the body.

In *Ce Sexe qui n'en est pas un*, Luce Irigary says that men see differently than women. "Woman takes pleasure more from touching than from looking, and her entry into a dominant scopic economy signifies, again, her consignment to passivity: she is to be the beautiful object of contemplation. While her body finds itself thus eroticized... her sexual organ represents *the horror of nothing to see*."[1]

Judith Butler, talking about the body and so about the act of seeing in her discussion of Irigaray's deconstruction of Plato's *Timaeus*, argues: "against those who would claim the body's irreducible materiality is a necessary precondition for feminist practice, I suggest that prized materiality may well be constituted through an exclusion and a degradation of the feminine that is profoundly problematic for feminism."[2]

If we are to talk about gender, first we must locate the body, first we must see whether or not the body is and is only material.

Butler further argues that if materiality is to be considered a basis for the body and so for gender, it must first be asked whether materiality is a ground. That is, the metaphysics in which materiality as ground lodges must be found, and the political concerns and aims that have lead to these metaphysics:

> If the body signified as prior to signification is an effect of signification, then the mimetic or representational status of language, which claims that signs follow bodies as their necessary mirrors, is not mimetic at all.[3]

I want to return to this key statement when I talk about language at the end of this essay.

Butler proceeds to demonstrate that an equation between the (female) body and materiality and the positing of that closure named *male/female* depends upon an exclusion of women. The "phallocentric economy . . . produces the 'feminine' as its constitutive outside. Matter is the site at which the feminine is excluded."[4] Women are excluded both as the improper and as the propertyless.

In his *Timaeus*, Plato divides generation into three parts: the process of generation, that in which generation takes place, and "that of which the thing generated is a resemblance naturally produced."[5] The generation source or spring is likened to a father; the receiving principle to a mother; the intermediate nature to a child. The child resembles the father, for both father and child possess the capability of mimesis. Whereas the woman, the receiver, cannot change, for she has no form and so can neither be named nor discussed.

She has no essence, for all that comes into being, according to Plato, partakes of form.

I knew this as a child, before I had ever read Plato, Irigaray, Butler. That, as a girl, I was outside the world. I wasn't. I had no name. For me, language was being. There was no entry for me into language. As a receptacle, as a womb, as Butler argues, I could be entered, but I could not enter, and so I could neither have nor make meaning in the world.

I was unspeakable so I ran into the language of others.

In this essay, as yet, I am only repeating those languages.

Though I couldn't be named, everyone was naming me: "This naming of what cannot be named is itself a penetration into this receptacle that is at once a violent erasure, one that establishes it as an impossible yet necessary site for all further inscriptions."[6] That is, the name *female* acts to erase the presence of women.

When I was a girl, I wanted to do anything but be a girl, for both *girl* and *woman* were the names of nothing.

Now that I am no longer nothing, now that I have run away

and so thrown off the names *girl* and *woman*, I am left not even with that. Not even with nothing. With a name such as *pirate* which seems solely metaphorical. And that isn't good enough. I want to *see* my body.

Searching for the body

When I was a girl, I ran into books. Like Alice in Lewis Carroll's *Through the Looking Glass*, a text which Irigaray turns to in her introduction to *Ce Sexe qui n'en est pas un*, I was asking "Who am I?"

Alice falls, as I do when I read this book, into a mirror-world, a text world, and there is presented with five poems and songs. New texts as opposed to the songs and lullabies she remembers. These five texts try to teach her who she is.

The first poem is found in a looking-glass book and so, to be comprehended, must be read in a mirror. A mirror of a mirror: a labyrinth. Though many of the meanings of the words of this poem "Jabberwocky" are ambiguous, its story is clear, simple.

Stanza 1: description of the natural world.
Stanza 2: a father warns his son to shun three different monsters.
Stanza 3: the son pursues the most monstrous of these monsters.
Stanza 4: suddenly, the main monster, the Jabberwock, appears.
Stanza 5: the son slays the Jabberwock.
Stanza 6: the father congratulates his killer son.
Stanza 7: whereupon nature is restored to herself. Or, to itself.

An Oedipal tale with a few interesting changes.

In the poem, the genders of the monsters are unknown; the major monster is an *it*. In the Greek myth and its reiterations, the monster is a Sphinx which, according to Robert Graves, had a woman's head, a lion's body, a snake's tail, and the wings of an eagle. Thus, in the Sphinx were united the female and animal worlds. As in related *monsters* or *wonders* such as Medusa. "Was Oedipus," asks Graves, "a thirteenth-century invader of Thebes, who suppressed the old Minoan cult of the goddess . . . ?"[7]

In the Oedipal myth, there are only two active females: the Sphinx, if the Sphinx is female, and Jocasta. Jocasta is not so much an actor as a site, the site for the wife-function and the mother-function. All else that we know about her is that she suicides: perhaps her only possible action in a male-dominated world. The Sphinx, one might note, fares not much better. Whereas in "Jabberwocky," there is no female, person, or site; there is only the *he* and the *it*. The *he* world is composed of humans; the *it* realm consists of nature and of the monstrous. One arises out of the other.

Since there's neither any antagonism between the men in "Jabberwocky," whereas in the Oedipal myth the murder of father by son is the core of the tale, nor are there any females, it is possible to draw a connection, as does Hesiod in his rendition of the Pandora myth, between the presence of the female and, if not patricide, at least male-to-male violence. The cliché would be that (hetero-) sexuality leads to violence between men.

In this sense, the center of "Jabberwocky," of that text the majority of whose words are ambiguous, is that which is missing.

Alice, in fact, doesn't understand this poem at all. More specifically, its perusal triggers the beginning of her confusion in looking-glass land.

As she continues traveling, her bewilderment increases. And so the child arrives in a woods where things have no name.

"What will become of *my* name when I go in?" asks Alice. When reading "Jabberwocky," she was confused about words relating to objects; now she can no longer find the meaning of words relating to the subject. To herself.

This woods is the beginning of the mirror of the mirror, of the labyrinth, in which all will be lost. Placing her hand on the trunk of one of those trees, she exclaims, "What *does* it call itself, I wonder? I do believe it's got no name . . ." And immediately she wonders, "And now, who am I?"

Luce Irigaray quoted this passage in the preface of *Ce Sexe qui n'en est pas un*: "I *will* remember," Alice continues, "if I can!" But she can't. All she knows is that who she is has to do with *L*.

Is it possible that the girl can find her actual body, and so what gender might be, in language? In a letter that, not yet language, has no discernible *mimetic* meaning?

Two "fat little men," Tweedledum and Tweedledee, present the second text, the second mirror. This charming poem, which echoes a bit of King Richard's speech in Shakespeare's *Richard II*, describes reality as a male-and-neuter world which is cannibalistic, moralistic, and hypocritical.

Remember that Lewis Carroll wrote *Through the Looking Glass* for a child.

In the fat boys' song, a Walrus and a Carpenter seduce a number of oyster children and, then, eat all of them up. Afterwards, the Walrus weeps.

Hearing this poem makes Alice doubt what she thinks is reality. Specifically, her reality. Does she, as Plato might put it, partake of essence, or is she just a figure in a man's dream? In the Oedipal dream? For, red, the King is (like) Oedipus after his slaughter of his father. And it is he who is dreaming Alice. "If that there King was to wake," explains Tweedledum to Alice, "you'd go out— bang!—just like a candle!"

After protesting her demise for less than a second, Alice comes up with this reply. "Besides, if *I'm* only a sort of thing in his dream, what are *you*, I should like to know?"

"Ditto," said Tweedledum.

"Ditto, ditto!" cried Tweedledee.

Leaving the reality brothers who are now doing just what an old song said they would do, Alice sojourns through a landscape whose perceptual objects keep shifting. Until she meets a man who can take care of her *reality* or *essence* problem.

Humpty Dumpty, a true egg-head and individualist, tells Alice: "When I choose a word, it means just what I want it to mean . . ." Then he presents the third text. In this poem, the narrator, who appears to be or mirrors Humpty, tries to tell some fishes what to do but they won't listen to him so he prepares to boil them alive. As he's trying to open the door to their bedroom so he can murder them all, the poem ends.

The main difference between this text and the previous one is that now the poem's speaker is first rather than third person. And so the terror of the world the poem is mirroring no longer is separate from the world outside the poem. Emphasising this terror, the egg-head's poem ends the way a dream ends when the dreamer/the dreamed is being chased by a murderer through sand. When the faster the dreamer tries to run, the more her feet get caught in those deepening, thickening sands . . .

Alice is searching for herself through texts of fear.

The Knight who, Alice had been told in the beginning of her journey, was destined to rescue her and bring her to sovereignty presents the next-to-last poem. Such is the nature of nights. He recites a song whose name is "Haddocks' Eyes."

Fish live next to the bodies of dead pirates.

"No," says the aged crumbled Knight. "The [poem's] name really is 'The Aged Aged Man.'"

He changes his name twice more.

Unlike the previous four texts, this poem does not tell a story. Beneath its fantastical surface, it is realistic: its content is that of an old man's experience of loneliness and poverty.

In his "Isa's Visit to Oxford," Lewis Carroll referred to himself as 'The Aged Aged Man.'"

When these songs are over, Alice becomes a queen. She has been initiated into language, into the reality of the world, for she has learned that, being female, she has no possible existence. So now she can be an adult:

"And what *is* this on my head?" she exclaimed in a tone of dismay, as she puts her hand up to something very heavy, that fitted tight all around her head . . .

"It was a golden crown."

The final text is the only one both spoken by a woman and which mentions women. In this song, Alice, once subject, becomes completely object or abject, for "hundreds of voices" describe her to herself. As mirror mirrors mirror, she learns her proper place in the world as I, as Alice's reader, thus as Alice, learn mine. I think that I, the reader, am a subject in the world until the White Queen warns me, in this world, things are reversed and subjects are not what they seem to be. "Which is easier to do," she asks Alice, "un-dish-cover the fish, or dishcover the riddle?"

Remember a joke in poor taste about smell and women.

The world is finally and fully nightmare. As soon as the song ends, Alice elects to destruct the world.

But she is only shaking a helpless kitten. She is destroying nothing. Can I escape by stopping reading?

I am Alice who ran into a book in order to find herself. I have found only the reiterations, the mimesis of patriarchy, or my inability to be. No body anywhere.

Who am I?

Has anybody seen gender?

Other than mimesis

There might be some clues to the White Queen's fish riddle in Butler's discussion of Irigaray's deconstruction of the *Timaeus*.

According to the Platonic model of generation, both the father and the child, the image of the father, possess the ability to repeat themselves. If language is seen as mimetic, they possess language.

But what if language need not be mimetic?

I am looking for the body, my body, which exists outside its patriarchal definitions. Of course, that is not possible. But who is any longer interested in the possible? Like Alice, I suspect that the body, as Butler argues, might not be co-equivalent with materality, that my body might deeply be connected to, if not be, language.

But what is this language? This language which is not constructed on hierarchical subject-object relations?

When I dream, my body is the site, not only of the dream, but also of the dreaming and of the dreamer. In other words, in this case or in this language, I cannot separate subject from object, much less from the acts of perception.

I have become interested in languages which I cannot *make up*, which I cannot *create* or even *create in*: I have become interested in languages which I can only come upon (as I disappear), a pirate upon buried treasure. The dreamer, the dreaming, the dream.

I call these languages, *languages of the body*.

There are, I suspect, a plurality or more of such languages. One such is the language that moves through me or in me or . . . for I cannot separate language body and identity . . . when I am moving through orgasm or orgasms. I shall give you an example. Nothing has been *made up* or *created*:

clear our forest water animals plants spout up twigs move twigs in lips go down under liquid comes out the animal there turns over
in safe place, center of. the tendrils are moving over the water. going down going deep and now the music begins only music is slow nothing happening in there where the trees grow. (there it's all happening.) just goes on and on what? nothing, for the body has taken over consciousness, is falling asleep as if in a faint, all pleasant here and quiet, lilac and grey, water mirrors air, long tall trees equal shadows. no difference. boat sails water like glass as long as there's no possibility of coming the coming is more violent keep on going because water and air mirrors endless therefore deep in there. the animals will come out the fur fur all lots of little animals can't stop now beep beep I'm going to find somewhere the gray going on there I go over again so there's green in the landscape this is so intense it can hardly be handled.
the treasure in the
midst of the
churning waters gold
dot
churn/separate all
around under in rolling
cylinders gets deeper
and deeper isn't bearable
such an opening cut the
whole earth disappearing
until all there's left is cries -oh oh oh oh no one knows
from what

the blackness
and afterwards the
repercussions
the very treasure—so horny for

Could gender lie here?

1995

Notes
1. Luce Irigary, *This Sex which is not One* (New York: Cornell University, 1985), p. 26.
2. Judith Butler, "Bodies That Matter," *Engaging With Irigaray*, eds, Burke, Schor, and Whitford (New York: Columbia University Press, 1994), p. 143.
3. Butler, p. 144.
4. Butler, p. 149.
5. Butler, p. 153.
6. Butler, p. 157.
7. Robert Graves, *The Greek Myths* (Rhode Island: Moyer Bell Limited, 1994), vol. 2, p. 13.

19. | The Future

1. Sterling

"You want to know what the future looks like?" Bruce Sterling asks in his new novel, *Holy Fire*. And answers his own question by saying, "I'll tell you. Look." At the end of this book, his main character, Mia or Maya, takes "her first true" camera shot and finally becomes what she wants to become, a photographer. What she manages by means of image, Sterling does via words: he pictures the future.

The future is one in which humans are so technologically advanced in the fields of virtual reality, body modification, and biochemistry that immortality is at the brink of being no longer imaginary. Mia, an old woman who is presented with the opportunity to look young again, does: she turns into a fashion model.

Is this every woman's dream? That is, a media or mediated or technological version of every woman's dream? Certainly, according to magazines such as *Vogue*. Which Sterling said he dutifully and not so dutifully read while researching his novel. Sterling's future, then, is the present, what is happening now but what we have not yet acknowledged or named.

Holy Fire, in the tradition of Philip K. Dick's work, is a realist novel: Sterling aims for the best type of journalism, that which allows us to see what we're not yet knowing we're seeing.

Isn't this what preachers do? "I'm a tech-pop-culture examiner," Sterling told me when I talked to him; "I'm now an elder statesman of cyberculture. I could have been a lawyer or a preacher, but I was too demented. But I'm not going to preach, to start my own cult. If I ever do that, you have permission to shoot me."

What does the future, that is the present, look like? Reality, for Sterling, is defined by society's technological status. The most interesting parts of *Holy Fire*, no surprise, are journalistic and pseudo-journalistic, factual and pseudo-factual:

> *The medical-industrial complex dominated the planet's economy. Biomedicine had the highest investment rates and the highest rates of technical innovation of any industry in the world . . . . In what had once been called the private sector, biomedicine was bigger than chemisynthesis, almost as big as computation.*

More realistic than science-fictional, yes?

When I asked Sterling what he thought about present fiction writing and which writers he was reading, he answered that, in order to research his novel, he devoured magazines, gun mags, mainly mags for and about women. Female bodybuilders and fashion models, Sterling commented, are cyborgs. They're made; they're more artificial than human. A female bodybuilder trains up to six hours a day solely due to vitamin supplementation (this isn't me speaking . . . as a former bodybuilder fan, I know that after forty five or so minutes of major training the glycogen level is too low to do much else besides stretching and aerobics). Sterling: "Both female bodybuilders and models are 105 % artificial. Mia is basically a cyborg.

Glamour is technologically induced and tech is all about glamour." We are now living in our future, in a media- or glamour-defined world, in cyborg reality, analyses Sterling.

"Are you making a moralistic point when you say this?" I asked Bruce, referring back to the archetype of Sterling-as-preacher.

"Absolutely not. This is just the way it is. Under the glamour and fashion and media rhetoric there's this intense medical rhetoric . . . . Look. The baby boomers who are running everything now, and they will in the years to come, are living on oatbran and exercise machines: they're vampires. When you turn fifty five, you should off yourself."

"You're not so young," I mumble. "Are you going to get rid of yourself?"

He laughs. "With any luck, I'll fall off a cliff." The tone of his voice changes. "It's different because I have children." Clearly, Sterling adores his children.

He informs me, and now I'm surprised, that he was also reading accounts of early-twentieth-century female artists for background for this novel. The biographies of Kiki de Montparnasse, Peggy Guggenheim; he mentions Djuna Barnes. I realize that his future cannot be just a description of technological society, for it has admitted within its venues historical accounts.

What does our future, in this case the presence of the Western white art world, look like when it is based upon technological reality and the biographical past? As in *Holy Fire*? At the end of the book, Maya is instructed that, ". . . artists today have every advantage. Education, Leisure. Excellent health. Free food, free shelter. Unlimited travel. All the time in the world to perfect their craft. All the information that the Net can feed them, the world's whole heritage of art. And what have they given us? Profoundly bad taste."

That this does not constitute an accurate description of the status of either art or the majority of artists in, for instance, the United States today is a minor consideration. What is more of interest is Maya's reply: "What do you want from them? Your world made them. Your world made me. What do you want from me?"

The real question is: what do we want from Sterling, from any novelist or artist who proposes to do more than make us cozy?

A more interesting question hides behind this one. Say that

artists are those who create. Are they gods, for God is she or he who creates. If society forms its artists and art, then the nature of that society forms the nature of art-making and of art in that society. Now could it be that a society seen through tech and based on tech, thus an art-making based on tech, is a reality that does not allow, as Rilke would have it, the creation of God?

This question is of importance to me, for it is we who must create the gods.

Somewhere during our discussion, Sterling announced, "A novel is not an experiment."

2. *Crash*—Cronenberg style

Last week I had the privilege of seeing *Crash*, David Cronenberg's film adaptation of James Ballard's novel. Unfortunately for me, I've only seen the film once; moreover, it could be that the distributors will pressure Cronenberg to edit out some of the more graphic sexual shots. I'm only guessing. Nevertheless I want to write about this movie now because what I saw was a masterpiece.

The film is not so much a conventional adaptation as a marriage between two of the most important artists working today, the kind of marriage that can take place only in the world depicted in and heralded by the movie itself, a world in which life and death collide and become one.

Whereas Ballard's novel begins in death, with the death of Vaughan, a car-crash fetishist and scientist, Cronenberg's movie begins with shot after shot of metal. Beautifully painted, gleaming metal. Kenneth Anger composed *Scorpio Rising,* a love song to motorcycles; this is Cronenberg's paean to cars. Just as husband and wife mirror each other, at least in alchemical terms, Cronenberg's sexual reiteration of metal images is a reenactment of Ballard's beginning-in-death.

These very first moments of the movie introduce a world in which desire equals death and vice-versa. In which death, and the approach to human death, is no longer an end but a beginning.

In the next paragraph of his novel, Ballard delves further into this new world: " . . . crushed bodies . . . like a haemorrhage of the sun." By using this image, he recalls Georges Bataille's sun-sports, splintering of the eye, the pineal eye, the asshole. Ballard turns to a surrealist, even an excommunicated one, the way Cronenberg does to the Anger of *Scorpio Rising*. Both do this in order to make clear that the territory of the car crash and of the crashed body is the realm of ecstasy.

This realm is future insofar as it is other; like Sterling's future, it has a presence/present we haven't yet acknowledged. Absolutely unlike Sterling's, it is a reality shaped by desire, a reality in which desire, especially sexual desire, turns into ecstasy.

Though Cronenberg's film, like Ballard's novel, has a simple narrative, poetry weighs on the narrative until its story is almost nonexistent.

What do I mean by "poetry"? I once asked a playwright, "What is the basis of a play, of theater?" I was trying to figure out how to write a play; I knew I didn't have a clue. He answered: Struggle. There has to be a protagonist and an antagonist because it's the tension between these two that constitutes drama. In *Crash*, there are no protagonists nor antagonists nor psychological drama: there is simply desire. The desire of the characters, the desire of the filmmaker. Every color in the film, every object as it is placed in space and next to other objects, the way that humans are seen as objects, how each frame moves to the next announces and repeats this desire. This is what I mean by "poetry." In Cronenberg's movie, all is crystal clear: the colors, the storyline, above all the intentions and emotions of the characters, a fictional Ballard, the filmmaker's intentions or desires. The fictional Ballard's longings and perceptions repeat Cronenberg's. It is repetition, not linear narrative, that shapes *Crash*; repetition, as Gertrude Stein noted, is the language of sexual love.

The name of the territory depicted by *Crash* is "violence," but then so is the name of this society in which I'm living. Art is metamorphosis: Cronenberg has transmuted my violent society into a world in which I want to be alive, in which I want to be human.

How has he done this? How can a world that is viable, unlike the nonviable society I know, be created? How can I, can we make

our existence's viable? In his novel, Ballard speaks of "the cele-
bration of wounds." He states: "For him [Vaughan] these wounds
were the keys to a new sexuality born from a perverse technology."
According to my lapsing memory, in the movie the fictional Ballard
says something like this to Vaughan, says that he and Vaughan
and their partners and lovers, almost all car crash survivors, are
recasting human sexuality and so, remodulating the human body
in the site or space of the meeting of human and metal, human and
technology. Sterling states something similar, but in his novel, in
terms of form and content, there is no ecstasy. No, Vaughan replies
to the fictional Ballard, that's too simple, that's only a beginning.

How can I, can we make the new world? How can we make
our world new? Further in his novel, Ballard comments that death
has "jerked loose" the sexual possibilities of everything around
him. As Cronenberg began the film with metal shot after metal
shot, his camera continues its sexual path by caressing each dis-
membered car crash limb, each far-flung body. The camera
transforms each wound into a new, never-before-seen genitalia.
After a car crash, anything can be penetrated, anyone, everything
and everyone is, anyone can penetrate and does. This new realm is
no longer one of duality, of men who penetrate with cocks and
women who get penetrated via cunts. Each car crash allows sexual
organs to proliferate everywhere: the world is sexualized as it was
when it began and in its constant beginnings.

How can the new world begin? It is the car crash, in other
words, it is death that allows us to transmute. I am in this society
living in a reality dominated by failed attempts to reject death, to
deny death's presence, while more and more of my friends are
dying. *Crash*, the film perhaps even more clearly than the book, is
the battle cry of those who are remaking sexuality, remaking our
perceptions. A battle cry and a slap in the face of rigid liberalism,
of those who refuse to acknowledge the body, sex, and death.

As I watched *Crash*, I watched my own desires and the ways I
desire, and I watched these change.

How can a film remake sex and sexuality if sexual desire lies
outside human control? (Perhaps the technological society, as in

Sterling, believes that the body and sex can be controlled. But then, what of death? This is one reason that sex must always be viewed in partnership with death.) I'll give you one example of what Cronenberg does in *Crash*. For me, the central shot of the film, a few seconds long, is one of a penis, I remember that it's Vaughan's, next to Katherine's, Ballard's wife's, cunt. The image immediately repeats itself as a finger in the same position on the cunt. What interested me most was that, contrary and probably antagonistic to all porn conventions, the cock is not hard. Through sexual desire, both his own and that of his characters, Cronenberg has reenvisioned the dominant and always rigid phallus of the old the king-must-not-die world as other, soft, another body part, by the end of the film as metal, a car, death, a kiss. In the last moments of the movie, the fictional Ballard promises his wife that he will be able to enact her most profound sexual desires by killing her in a car crash.

A slap in the face of the white Western world.

Making, the reenvisioning of sexuality, the making of a new world is personal. Ballard's novel is a love letter to Vaughan. "He knew that as long as he provoked me with his own sex, which he used casually as if he might discard it for ever," says Ballard, "I would never leave him." In Cronenberg's film, Vaughan and the fictional Ballard have sex; the whole film, actually, is Cronenberg's fucking of Ballard. To desire to do is to do and to do is to desire to do in this world which is no longer dualistic.

In *Crash*, Cronenberg has made the gods.

3.

I'd like to say something personal about these two approaches toward picturing the future, for as I write this I am sitting here, fighting off cancer. If we envision, as our possible future, our presence, a reality and society that is only technological, we are killing off ourselves. Rilke's last poem in his *Books of Hours* has the same colors as Cronenberg's film:

. . . like a holy face
held in my dark hands.

1996

Gary Indiana's essays, like his fiction, take no prisoners. In his fifteen years of writing cultural criticism, he has altered the way we look at ourselves and our society. Ignoring good taste, Indiana writes discomforting home truths, because his views of home are unique and never comfortable. His insights are acute, brash, bracing, intelligent; his subjects and speculations range from Rodney King's beating to Mary McCarthy's friendship with Hannah Arendt to the presidential campaign of 1992. *Let It Bleed* collects for the first time some of the most engaging, provocative, and exciting writing that has been seen and produced in a long time.

'His reports from the front ring as true as stories your grandma told you a hundred times, except that your grandma wasn't this funny, smart, mean, self-examined or perceptive—nor, in all probability, did she use the same vocabulary.'

Publishers Weekly

Steven Shaviro

Doom Patrols

Doom Patrols is a rollercoaster ride through late-20th-century culture. Considering topics as diverse as Elvis worship, the erotics of cyberspace, fantasies of the millennium, multiple personality syndrome, and the molecular logic of insect DNA; ranging from William Burroughs to Dean Martin, from Michel Foucault to My Bloody Valentine, from Andy Warhol to Bill Gates, the essays in this collection take an idiosyncratic look at the forces and counter-forces currently transforming American and world culture.

Jonathan Romney

Short Orders

The nineties has been a turbulent and changing period for cinema. The film critic Jonathan Romney has spent the decade at the pictures making sense of things. *Short Orders* is a collection of his sharp, inquiring and entertaining writings on film, from art house to multiplex, and featuring his unique take on the likes of Tarantino, Jarman, Scorsese and Almodóvar. The collection also includes extended reflections on the end of cinema's first century and Hollywood's entry into the digital age and, with it, the end of the reign of the 'real' on-screen.

'I've long felt that Jonathan Romney was one of the sharpest film critics writing in English. Reading his collected pieces in *Short Orders* has confirmed and deepened this feeling. Moving with breathtaking confidence, from the American mainstream to the more obscure byways of World Cinema, *Short Orders* is bursting with dazzling and provocative observations. Written with verve, bold intelligence and dead pan wit, *Short Orders* is the most exhilarating collection of film criticism in a very long time.'

Howard Schuman

Lynne Tillman

The Broad Picture

Lynne Tillman's essays are irreverent, smart, funny – evidence of her playful, rebellious mind. They are collected here together for the first time. Her subjects range broadly and wildly, from Matisse and 'reading women' to the issue of race in *The Bodyguard*, from Ray Charles' voice and lyrics to narrative theories, from cat therapy to sex, memory and death. An exceptional writer, Tillman takes the reader on an expansive tour of 20th century life and culture to unearth and enlighten its preoccupations, fears and obsessions.

'Adding to her daring feats in fiction, Lynne Tillman is now an essayist for our times. A private eye in the public sphere, she refuses no assignment and distils the finest wit, intelligence and hard evidence from some of the world's most transient artifacts and allegories. This is a truly memorable book.'

Andrew Ross,
author of 'The Chicago Gangster Theory of Life'

'Tillman's work is always intelligent, always subtle, and very often funny, and the scalpel she uses for slicing it into the American order of things has a decidedly wicked edge to it.'

Patrick McGrath